THE FOUR
CORNERSTONES
OF PEACE

VERA MICHELES DEAN

THE FOUR CORNERSTONES OF PEACE

Whittlesey House

McGRAW-HILL BOOK COMPANY, INC.
New York   *London*

First Printing

PUBLISHED BY WHITTLESEY HOUSE
A division of the McGraw-Hill Book Company, Inc.

Printed in the United States of America

TO
ELINOR AND BILLY
AND OTHER BUILDERS OF TOMORROW

When wilt thou save the people?
O God of mercy, when?
Not kings and lords, but nations!
Not thrones and crowns, but men!
Flowers of thy heart, O God, are they!
Let them not pass, like weeds, away!
Their heritage a sunless day!
God save the people!

EBENEZER ELLIOTT, *The People's Anthem*

FOREWORD

HERE, on still August evenings when the shadows lengthen over the green hills, and later, when a dazzling moon silvers the inky waters of the lake, both the destructive force released by the atomic bomb and the constructive hopes emerging from the San Francisco conference seem equally remote. But there was beauty, too, and peace in the woods and lakes of Finland in the golden days of my childhood, the days of August, 1914; and breathtaking loveliness in sunsets over the fjords of Norway, where I heard the news of Poland's invasion by Germany in September, 1939. Which is reality—the smoking shambles of Hiroshima and the subhuman brutalities of Buchenwald and the Death March of Bataan, or the discussions around the green table of men and women striving to create an effective international organization? Or is reality none of these, but the quiet, undramatic efforts of people everywhere to keep body and soul together, to find solace in love and friendship, and to capture, if only for a moment, a sense of the glory and exaltation of living?

All these, the evil and the glory, the love and hate, are part of human experience. But we shall find no surcease, we shall betray our children, unless we continue to fight, with the same determination that we have shown on the battlefield, the forces that bring about war—poverty and disease, the frustration that springs from unemployment, the greed for power and advantage that can corrupt the healthiest nation, the fear that destroys reason. In this struggle we cannot look for unconditional surrender. It is a struggle that will go on as long as there is life on earth—but in which victory will belong to those who prevent, not to those who win, wars between nations.

To the Foreign Policy Association, and especially to General Frank R. McCoy, who has generously encouraged me in every task I have undertaken during the war years, I owe warm thanks for permission to use in this book some materials prepared for FPA publications. I am also deeply grateful to my colleague, Olive Holmes, who made a major contribution to the chapter on the Mexico City conference.

VERA MICHELES DEAN

August 31, 1945,
Lake Morey, Fairlee, Vermont.

CONTENTS

		PAGE
PREFACE: A JOB TO BE DONE		xi
CHAPTER		
I.	THE DUMBARTON OAKS CONFERENCE	1
II.	THE YALTA CONFERENCE	25
III.	THE MEXICO CITY CONFERENCE	39
IV.	THE SAN FRANCISCO CONFERENCE	53
V.	POTSDAM AND AFTER	104
VI.	THE AMERICAN VOTER AND INTERNATIONAL ORGANIZATION	124
TEXTS OF DOCUMENTS		143
INDEX		261

PREFACE: A JOB TO BE DONE

IN THE turbulent years ahead, many of us may ponder the last words of Socrates when, after his condemnation to death by the judges of Athens, he said: "The hour of departure has arrived, and we go our ways—I to die, and you to live. Which is better God only knows."

Terrible as the sufferings inflicted by war on millions of men, women and children have been, the problems of those who live to take part in the tasks of post-war reconstruction will be an even greater test of courage, vision, and the capacity to work together for the common good. The ashes of Stalingrad and Warsaw, of Rotterdam and Cologne, of Cassino and Manila have not yet been cleared away; yet already new animosities and fresh distrust loom among nations who were expected to continue into the days of peace the cooperation they had achieved in time of war. As British Foreign Secretary Eden said at San Francisco, there is a job of work to be done in achieving peace.

Security: Our Primary Task

What is the primary task that awaits us as we clear up the débris of war? The primary task of the United Nations is to answer the question that is haunting men and women everywhere—the question of how to achieve security now that hostilities are over. This is a twofold task. People want to have security at home, against the specter of unemployment that stalked all lands during the inter-war years; and security abroad, against the renewal of armed aggression. These two aspects of security are inextricably linked. We know now that we shall be unable to enjoy peace and prosperity within our borders if the rest of the world is torn by war and civil strife, and overshadowed by hunger, misery, and disease. Sooner or later the repercussions of events abroad would be felt here, as they have in two world wars. It is therefore not for reasons of sentiment alone, or idealism alone, but for reasons of self-interest that the United States is concerned with plans for post-war security.

The Lone-Hand Way

How shall we go about achieving security? The old time-tested way, which has been used again and again throughout history, is for every nation to try to assure its own security by its own unaided efforts, regardless of what happens to the rest of the world. This way is open today only to the great powers. The small nations have neither the territory, the manpower, nor the industrial and financial resources to defend themselves against attack by strong, aggressive neighbors. But let us assume that the United States, Britain, and Russia could achieve security by their own national efforts. This, you might say, would be worth trying if the great powers at least can gain security for five, or ten, or twenty years. What must they do to achieve security by this method?

Great powers who are determined to rely on their own national efforts for security usually try to do two things. First, they try to create zones of security around their territories by taking over or dominating adjoining areas. For example, when Russia claims eastern Poland, the Baltic states, and bases in Finland, she claims them not chiefly on

historic grounds, although she could do so since these territories were part of the Russian Empire for varying periods
of time before 1917. She claims these areas on grounds
of security, to cushion the shock of future German aggression. As long as we live in a world of international anarchy,
every nation is like a man on a trapeze—afraid to let go of
the foothold of national security until it is sure of international security. Russia's claims are understandable claims.

The Struggle for Safety Zones

The danger, however, is that every great power can make
similar claims. Although the British have not yet done so
officially, they could reasonably say that they need the
Italian colonies in Africa conquered by British troops during
this war; also bases in the Low Countries to protect their
Channel ports; and in Italy and Greece to protect their life-
line through the Mediterranean. Then, too, Americans can
say—and some have said already—that the United States
should take over as many islands in the Pacific as possible
to guard us against any future attack by Japan. Other Americans go further and say that we should actually take over
the possessions of our allies—Britain, Holland, and France—
in the Western Hemisphere, so as to make this country im-
pregnable to attack also in the Atlantic Ocean. Thus if each
great power demands territories it believes it needs for national security, a dangerous race will have started for re-
division of the world's goods. Such a race would have only
one predictable outcome: another world war, this time among
the victors in this war for the spoils of victory.

But, you might say, this would not be so dangerous as it
seems, because every great power would maintain armed

forces sufficient to ward off attack from any quarter. There is no doubt that in future years Britain and the Dominions, the United States, and Russia could attempt to maintain armed forces more or less equivalent to those they have raised in time of war. Nor does any responsible person today urge the disarmament of the United Nations. The only disarmament that is being discussed is that of Germany and Japan. But the question with which we are faced is whether every great power will remain armed to the teeth after the war, ready to take on all comers, and ready too to pay the high cost of such armaments; or whether each will gradually reduce its armaments, thus reducing also the economic burdens borne by its people. Should nations decide to follow the second course, they could then pool their reduced armaments in a common force placed at the disposal of an international organization.

Let us assume, however, that every great power decides to maintain its own armed forces on a basis comparable to that of wartime. What would this mean for its people? If we are to maintain in time of peace armed forces comparable to our wartime forces, which cost us millions of dollars every day, we shall have to bid farewell to social progress. And sooner or later we shall discover that we have accepted the very philosophy of life we are fighting—the philosophy that forces the individual to become an instrument, a slave of a totalitarian state whose sole aim is military preparedness.

Grim as this prospect may seem, some people might say it is worth considering if the great powers can thus hope to achieve security. But is mere possession of additional territory and vast armaments in itself a safeguard of national security? If they are, then why did Germany and Japan prove insecure? Germany achieved maximum expansion on the European continent, including European Russia, and built up the mightiest land forces of modern times. Yet the Germans found themselves driven out of the countries they conquered, faced with the necessity of defending themselves on their own soil. This was a contingency so feared by the German Army in 1918 that, rather than permit the Allies to invade Germany, Ludendorff at that time insisted on seeking an armistice. Japan too seemed for a time to have conquered a vast empire in Asia, rich with many of the raw materials it coveted for the development of its industrial and military machine. Yet the conquest of large sections of China, the occupation of the Dutch East Indies and the Philippines, the control of Burma and Malaya, and the possession of land, naval, and air forces did not make the Japanese safe in their home islands. With the development of long-range bombing; with the perfecting of such ruthless instruments of war as the atomic bomb; with the proof, so brilliantly given by Americans, that the armies of one nation can cross oceans to invade the shores of other nations, it is doubtful that any country will in the future be long invulnerable to attack.

The Way of Collective Action

It is because there is so little hope that any country, no matter how powerful, will be able to achieve security by its own unaided efforts that people everywhere have sought an alternative method. What is the alternative? It can best be described by that much derided phrase—collective security. This phrase had come into disrepute because many people mistakenly assumed that the League of Nations was a system of collective security. Since the League had failed to prevent World War II, they jumped to the conclusion that collective security had proved a failure.

Yet most of us realize today that the League of Nations was not a system of collective security. It was an agglomeration of nations, each of which was so jealous of its sovereign rights that it refused to make any major adjustments for the sake of the international community as a whole. If all that we can produce at the end of this war is a replica of the League, then it might perhaps be better not to establish such an organization. It would be better not to create the illusion again that merely by signing some documents we have assured peace on earth, thus lulling people into a false sense of security. It would be more merciful to let every nation rely, as in the past, on its own military power for such precarious safety as it might attain in a world in which, to quote Hobbes' famous phrase, human life would be "nasty, brutish and short."

What Makes International Organization Effective?

If we are to build on stronger foundations this time, what should an international organization have in order to be effective? Such an organization should be able to do at least two things. First, there should be continuous consultation among nations about any friction or dispute which might lead to war, if not alleviated or settled. Infrequent conferences held in the full spotlight of world publicity do not fill the need for day-to-day consideration of problems likely to provoke conflict—the kind of consideration that we give to local problems in city and village councils and to the problems of the nation in Congress and the Executive Departments. The League of Nations made only partial provision for such consultation. Second, to be effective, an international organization should have military force at its disposal, to be used whenever a nation resorts to aggression after its legitimate grievances have been given due consideration and a genuine attempt has been made to meet them. The League of Nations had no such force at its disposal.

There are many sincere and high-minded people who believe that the use of force should be eliminated in human relations. Yet those who object to the use of force among nations do not usually demand the removal of the police from our villages, towns, and states. Of course, the police in this country and in other civilized countries are themselves under the control of a government—municipal, state, or national—and can be checked by the courts. Thus the police for the most part are not apt to make arbitrary and violent use of force, as nations have done again and again in their relations with each other. However, the answer to this point is not that we should eliminate the use of force in relations between nations, but that we should place such force under the control of an international government and subject it to check by an international court.

Many people deplore the necessity of using force in international relations and are skeptical about political adjustments of international problems. They wonder whether it might not be possible to settle all conflicts among nations through an international court. Such a court, as stated in the San Francisco Charter and previously in the League of Nations Covenant, is an essential feature of any international organization. But a court alone could not possibly be expected to settle all conflicts among nations. In our nation we do not rely solely on the courts to adjust relations among our citizens. In addition to courts we have the political machinery of the Executive and Congress and the enforcement machinery of our police.

Also, most of the conflicts among nations that are likely to lead to war are not what we call "justiciable" conflicts. That is, they often concern matters on which there are as yet no accepted rules of international law and which therefore cannot be settled by a court administering law. What an international court can do is to decide questions involving the interpretation of treaties; that is one of the principal sources of what we call international law. However, treaties and other legal documents cover only a few of the problems that lead to conflicts among nations. For example, the hostility of some Germans toward Poland was a very real factor in unleashing World War II, but it was an intangible matter that could not be embodied in a lawyer's brief or passed on by a court. Or take Mussolini's claim that Italy was a poor country which should increase its resources by armed expansion; that was an important reason for Italy's invasion of Ethiopia, but it was not a question a court could have decided.

Most of the reasons for which nations go to war are political, economic, social, or psychological in character, or a mixture of all these. They must be dealt with by international institutions equipped to settle political, economic, and social questions, staffed preferably by men and women who have some knowledge and understanding of the psychology and emotions of the various peoples involved. When disputes of this kind fail to be settled by peaceful means, and an act of aggression occurs, an international court would not be prepared to meet such an emergency. Then force will have to be used by the international organization as a last resort.

No Millennium in Store

Even if we do succeed in establishing an effective international organization, we must not expect it to bring about the millennium. Many people believe that the moment an international organization has been set up it will assure "order" throughout the world. But as long as there is life on earth there will be disorder, there will be constant changes in the relations of human beings with each other. Our task is not to prevent all conflicts among nations (that is impossible), but to make sure that when conflicts do arise they are settled by peaceful means, not by war. Again, some people think that an international organization will be no good unless it can find "solutions" for all problems that may arise between nations. No one familiar with the ways of mankind can possibly believe that there are finite "solutions" for any problem. The best we can do is to reach workable compromises, knowing full well that any compromise made today will have to be revised tomorrow. Human institutions grow very slowly. Just remember how long it took for democratic institutions to develop from Magna Carta to the present day. Viewed in the perspective of history, our experience with international organization is very brief.

At this point pessimists are apt to say, "What's the use of even discussing an international organization? There have always been wars, and there always will be wars. So let's just accept this unpleasant situation as gracefully as possible." Such an attitude is not only defeatist, but it also falsifies the historical experience of mankind. Let us look back for a moment to the feudal period in Europe, to our own frontier days in this country. In those times the individual felt that he had a sacred right of self-defense; and, to defend himself and his family against all comers, he carried a lance, sword, pistol, or shotgun. Then, gradually, so gradually that it is impossible to fix definite dates, the individual began to wonder whether he might not achieve greater security by entrusting his protection and that of his family to the community; whether he might gain more than he would lose by foregoing his sacred right of self-defense. And he began to leave his lance, sword, pistol, or shotgun at the door of the courthouse and the council chamber. Thus individuals gave up what they had once regarded as their right, and instead worked together to establish peaceful national communities in which conflicts are settled not by duels or private feuds, but by legislation, by the decisions of the courts, by the use of police force against the few who in any community on occasion defy the law.

Today nations are at the stage where individuals were in feudal times and in the days of our frontier. Optimists had assumed that in international affairs we had reached the twentieth century because we had learned to use so many of this century's technical gadgets. Pessimists would say that internationally we are still in the jungle age. But let us be moderately cheerful and say that nations today are facing the decisions that confronted individuals in olden days. Nations must decide whether they will gain more than they will lose by entrusting their protection, in part at least, to an international organization. Will they leave their guns and bombs outside the doors of courthouses and council chambers? This is a difficult decision to make, and it may not be fully reached in our lifetime. But it will be made some time in human history. Every small thing we can do now to advance this decision is a great step forward, even though it may seem insignificant to us who are so close to the affairs of our times that we cannot see this century in true perspective.

The Four Conferences

An attempt to set up the machinery of an effective international organization was made at the San Francisco conference, which opened on April 25, 1945. At this conference fifty United Nations drew up a charter based on proposals drafted at Dumbarton Oaks, near Washington, August 21–October 7, 1944, by representatives of the United States, Britain, Russia and China. An important gap left in the Dumbarton Oaks proposals concerning voting procedure in the Security Council was filled in at the Yalta conference, February 4–12, 1945. There President Roosevelt, Prime Minister Churchill and Marshal Stalin, representing the Big Three, considered a wide range of problems raised by the impending defeat of Germany. Subsequently, representatives of the United States and nineteen Latin American countries (with the exception of Argentina) met in Mexico City, February 21–March 8, 1945. There the historic Act of Chapultepec was adopted, providing for defense of the regional security of the Western Hemisphere during the war, and foreshadowing the adoption of similar measures in the post-war period.

This book analyzes the documents on international organization that issued from the four conferences of Dumbarton Oaks, Yalta, Mexico City, and San Francisco. It seeks to answer the questions most frequently asked about them by men and women throughout this country—men and women who, as voters, will finally have to pass judgment on the steps the United States will take to implement the Charter of the United Nations organization. Our people, like the people of the other United Nations, have expended blood, sweat, and tears in fighting a war of survival. They are entitled to receive forthright answers to the questions they are anxiously asking about prospects for post-war security, about possible safeguards that may be adopted to prevent the recurrence of a world catastrophe in another ten or twenty years. The time is not yet ripe for a definitive study of the conferences that are the four cornerstones of the international organization we are endeavoring to build. But human beings whose destiny is being shaped by the day-to-day developments of this critical period cannot wait for definitive volumes by historians who will ultimately have access to records and memoirs unavailable now. They want and need to understand the significance of long-term trends behind the headlines, and it is their need that this book attempts to fill.

The four conferences discussed here have only laid the cornerstones for the international structure. The structure itself remains to be built and expanded in the future to meet new needs as they arise. The conferences have furnished us with tools. Now we must learn how to use these tools in fixing post-war problems. Some of these problems, such as territorial settlements, have already been tackled, notably in the armistices concluded by the Big Three (the Soviet Union acting on their behalf) with Germany's satellites in Eastern Europe—Finland, Rumania, Bulgaria and Hungary—and in the agreement reached at Yalta to recognize the Curzon Line, with minor rectifications, as the border between Russia and Poland. Others have been discussed by various Allied commissions—for example, the treatment of Germany by the now disbanded European Advisory Commission in London, composed of representatives of the United

States, Britain, Russia and France, the problem of German reparations by a Reparations Commission in Moscow, and the treatment of war criminals by the War Crimes Commission in London.

Problems of food and nutrition were considered at Hot Springs, and relief and rehabilitation at Atlantic City, in 1943; education in London in April, 1944; monetary and financial questions at Bretton Woods in July, 1944; civil aviation in Chicago in November–December, 1944. The technical agencies established or projected at these conferences were the Food and Agriculture Organization, the United Nations Relief and Rehabilitation Administration, the International Bank for Reconstruction and Development, the International Monetary Fund, the Organization for Educational and Cultural Reconstruction, and the Interim Council on Civil Aviation. All these are to be fitted into the framework of the Economic and Social Council of the United Nations organization established at San Francisco. Their success or failure will depend on the success or failure of the United Nations to maintain and strengthen the security machinery officially blueprinted in the San Francisco Charter.

Time alone can answer the most far-reaching question that can be asked about this machinery. Is it sufficiently broad in conception to cope with the conflicts of ideas— reminiscent of the struggle between paganism and Christianity, between feudalism and the Industrial Revolution— that are tearing mankind apart in our century? Efforts to protect human rights, so cruelly abused in this war, call for international action, as do the problems of colonial peoples and the need for social and economic reforms which, if not met, may provoke revolutions that in turn will bring about

reactionary movements pregnant with future wars. The
United Nations organization must be strong enough to channel the red-hot lava of controversy about the ends and
means of human society which is now pouring out in every
quarter of the globe, often threatening to engulf what we
have known as civilization. No document can of itself do
the job. As John Mason Brown has said in *Many a Watchful
Night,* the making of the peace will require great character
and great characters.

The task of achieving international security and general
welfare cannot be accomplished by a few men, no matter
how well-intentioned or farsighted they may be. It will require the efforts of all of us to carry it through. The building of an effective international organization could become,
for the twentieth century, what the building of a cathedral
was for the Middle Ages—"ennobled by one of the greatest group aspirations of the race in one of those high tides
of creative energy that rise only at rare intervals out of the
ocean of time." * And like the selfless builders of cathedrals,
most of whom remained anonymous, we must learn to blend
"art and engineering and functionalism with the aspiration
and the dream."

* Robert G. Anderson, *The Biography of a Cathedral.* New York, Longmans,
Green & Co., 1944.

CHAPTER I

THE DUMBARTON OAKS CONFERENCE

August 21–October 7, 1944

THE Dumbarton Oaks conference, held at a historic mansion in Washington from August 21 to October 7, 1944, consisted of two phases. During the first phase, representatives of the United States, Britain and Russia conferred about problems of world security organization. During the second phase, the representatives of the United States and Britain discussed the same problems with representatives of China, since Russia, who was not at that time at war with Japan, had preferred not to sit in at the conference with China. The United States delegation was headed by Edward R. Stettinius, Jr., then Acting Secretary of State; that of Britain by Sir Alexander Cadogan, Under Secretary of State for Foreign Affairs; that of Russia by Andrei Gromyko, Russian Ambassador to Washington; and that of China by V. K. Wellington Koo, Chinese Ambassador to Great Britain.

Ten Key Points

So far as the published record shows, the Dumbarton Oaks conferees concentrated their attention on the problems of establishing the machinery of international security organization and, unlike the Yalta conferees, did not attempt to cover the wide range of political problems created by the war. Here are the ten key points on which they reached agreement:

1. There should be established an international organization to be known as The United Nations. Its main purpose should be "to maintain international peace and security." To that end it should "take effective collective measures for the prevention and removal of threats to the peace and the suppression of acts of aggression or other breaches of the peace, and to bring about by peaceful means adjustment or settlement of international disputes which may lead to a breach of the peace." Membership should be open to all "peace-loving" states. The organization should have four principal organs: a General Assembly, a Security Council, an international court of justice, and a Secretariat.

2. The General Assembly should be composed of representatives of all nations who are members of the organization. The Assembly should have functions in two fields: in the field of security, it should consider the general principles of cooperation in the maintenance of peace and security; and in the field of economic and social cooperation it should "facilitate solutions of international, economic, social, and other humanitarian problems and promote respect for human rights and fundamental freedoms." The Assembly, however, cannot recommend any action in the sphere of security, which is reserved to the Security Council. Important decisions of the Assembly are to be taken by a two-thirds majority of those present and voting. Other decisions are to be made by a simple majority vote.

3. The Security Council, the kernel of the proposed organization, should be charged with the task of maintaining peace and security. According to the Dumbarton Oaks proposals, it is to be composed of one representative of each of

eleven nations. Five of these nations—the United States, Britain, Russia, China, and "in due course" France, which are regarded as great powers—are to be permanent members of the Security Council. The six others are to be elected by the General Assembly for a term of two years each. The Security Council should be so organized as to be able to function continuously. The question of voting procedure in the Security Council was not settled, and was stated to be "still under consideration."

4. The Security Council should be empowered to investigate any dispute, or any situation which may lead to international friction or give rise to a dispute. If the nations involved in a dispute have failed to settle it by peaceful means such as diplomatic negotiation, mediation, conciliation, arbitration, or judicial settlement by the international court of justice, then the Security Council should take any measures necessary for the maintenance of international peace and security. To give effect to its decisions, the Security Council should be able to apply a whole range of measures that do not involve the use of armed force. These could be complete or partial interruption of rail, sea, air, postal, telegraphic, radio, and other means of communication, and the severance of diplomatic and economic relations with any nation that threatens the peace.

5. Should these nonmilitary measures prove inadequate, the Security Council should be able to take such action by air, naval, or land forces as may be necessary to maintain or restore international peace and security. For this purpose every member of the proposed organization should undertake to make the necessary armed forces available to the Security Council, in accordance with a special agreement or agreements. Every member of the United Nations will be

expected to conclude an agreement stating the numbers and types of armed forces and the nature of the facilities and assistance it shall place at the disposal of the Security Council.

6. The use of the forces made available by the United Nations should be decided by the Security Council, with the advice and assistance of a Military Staff Committee responsible to it. The Military Staff Committee is to be composed of the Chiefs of Staff of the United States, Britain, Russia, China, and France, or their representatives, with provision for the participation of other states when necessary.

7. In addition to the armed forces which the members of the United Nations are to hold in readiness for use by the Security Council, air force contingents should also be immediately available to the Council for urgent military tasks. With the development of long-range bombing, and the perfecting of such weapons as the robot bomb, it was felt by the Dumbarton Oaks conferees that the Security Council should have at its disposal air force units that could be used without delay against an aggressor nation.

8. Nothing in the Dumbarton Oaks document precludes the existence of regional arrangements or agencies for dealing with matters relating to the maintenance of international peace and security appropriate for regional action, provided —and this is a fundamental condition—that such arrangements or agencies are consistent with the purposes and principles of the organization. In other words, there would be no objection to such agencies as the Pan American Union, or to the mutual aid alliances between Britain and Russia, and France and Russia—on condition that they function within, not outside, the framework of the United Nations and conform to the basic conditions of the charter of the organization.

9. The proposed organization is to include, as its principal judicial organ, an international court of justice modeled on the Permanent Court of International Justice established in 1919.

10. While problems of military security should be handled by the Security Council, economic, social, and other humanitarian problems should be handled by the General Assembly and, under its authority, by the Economic and Social Council. This council should consist of representatives of eighteen member nations elected by the General Assembly for terms of three years each. Decisions of this council should be taken by simple majority vote of those present and voting. The council is intended to serve as an over-all coordinating body for any economic or social agencies that already exist or that may be formed in the future, and are brought into relationship with the organization.

How Did Dumbarton Oaks Compare with the League Covenant?

Because there had been such widespread disappointment with the inability of the League of Nations to prevent World War II, many people skeptically asked whether the Dumbarton Oaks proposals represented any improvement on the League Covenant. How did the proposed United Nations organization differ from the League? In what respects did it resemble that body?

To begin with, it is important to note that the United Nations were further along by 1944 in their plans for an international organization than was true of the Allies at a comparable stage of World War I. While nations were still under the shock of war and goaded by the threat of disaster, we were all trying to establish an international organization to make some adjustments and compromises for the common good. This in itself was a great step forward. And the United States had already committed itself to participation in an international organization by signing the Moscow Declaration of October 30, 1943, which was approved in the Connally resolution adopted by the Senate on November 5 of that year, and by summoning and taking an active part in the Dumbarton Oaks conference.

That conference, moreover, benefited by the experience of the League of Nations—an experience that was not available to the drafters of the League Covenant in 1919, who had to start from scratch. In 1944 plans were already being discussed for transfer to the United Nations organization of the archives and some of the organs and personnel of the League. So we started with a valuable backlog of machinery, as well as knowledge of what makes it work and what may cause it to break down. Our task was to carry forward the League's achievements in little-publicized fields such as health, economics, transit, and opium control. We also had to correct the grave weaknesses the League displayed in such matters as enforcement of security measures and adjustment of economic and social problems that threaten peace.

Dumbarton Oaks Structure More Flexible

When we compare the 1944 document with that of 1919, we notice that the Dumbarton Oaks proposals, unlike the League Covenant, did not contain a long list of fundamental principles about international problems such as disarmament, the treatment of backward peoples, labor or health conditions, traffic in women and children, and in opium, and others. Some critics felt for this reason that the Dumbarton

Oaks proposals were more narrow in scope than the League Covenant. In answer it was argued that the very fact that the Dumbarton Oaks document did not attempt to define in advance fundamental principles (which, through our failure to foresee all future problems, might some day develop into restrictions on the activities of the United Nations organization) actually made it more flexible than the League Covenant, more adaptable to changing circumstances. Those who took this view pointed out that many of the matters listed at length in the Covenant were included among the powers of the General Assembly and, under its authority, of the Economic and Social Council.

In contrast to the League Covenant, the Dumbarton Oaks document contained no undertaking concerning maintenance of existing boundaries such as the much-disputed Article 10 of the Covenant, by which League members pledged themselves "to respect and preserve as against external aggression the territorial integrity and existing political independence of all Members of the League." This article proved a bone of contention in the United States in 1919. In 1944, at a time when Europe and Asia were in the midst of seismic conflicts whose ultimate territorial results were as yet unpredictable, it was a sound decision not to tie down the international organization in advance to any particular boundary settlement. Nor was the Dumbarton Oaks document linked, like the League Covenant, to any peace settlement that might be reached at the close of hostilities. This was a distinct advantage, for the influence of the League had been weakened by the fact that the Covenant was made an integral part of the various peace treaties. As these treaties gradually fell into disrepute, so did the Covenant.

More Emphasis on Security

Another distinction between the two documents was that the Dumbarton Oaks proposals were far more definitely focused on the issue of security than the League Covenant. In Article 16 of the Covenant—another article that aroused bitter controversy in the United States in 1919—responsibility for action against an aggressor was divided between the individual members and the League Council, which had no military power at its disposal. In the Dumbarton Oaks proposals responsibility was centralized in the hands of the Security Council, which was to have at its disposal, as we have seen, air force contingents of the United Nations for immediate emergency action, plus armed forces, facilities, and installations provided by the member nations under special agreements.

The Dumbarton Oaks document did not attempt to define what constitutes aggression. Attempts to arrive at a generally acceptable definition during the inter-war years had proved futile. The suggestion had been made that the crossing of a country's frontier by the armed forces of another nation constitutes aggression. But this definition is obviously insufficient, for we all know from the experience of Manchuria, Ethiopia, and Poland that military invasion is but the last stage in a long-drawn-out process of provocation and pressure by non-military measures such as propaganda and economic restrictions. The Security Council proposed at Dumbarton Oaks was not hobbled by any specific definition of aggression that might be evaded by subtle interpretation of words. On the contrary, the range of circumstances under which the Council might act was very broad, embracing all kinds of conflicts among nations that threaten a breach of peace. The range of measures it was empowered to take, as we have seen, included many forms of non-military action, as well as the use of military force.

The Dumbarton Oaks document rightly emphasized not only the need for prompt and effective collective action against an aggressor, but also, to a greater extent than the League Covenant, stressed the need for continuous consultation among nations to prevent the development of situations that might threaten peace. Instead of leaving each member nation free to decide just how it would proceed to fulfill its undertakings against an aggressor as did the League Covenant, the Dumbarton Oaks document provided for agreements by which nations would place specified armed forces at the disposal of the Security Council. By creating the Economic and Social Council, the Dumbarton Oaks document also went further than the League Covenant in attempting to integrate existing international agencies and such agencies as might be established in the future to deal with economic and social problems. Moreover, it placed the proposed international court of justice within the framework of the United Nations organization, instead of leaving it outside as the Permanent Court of International Justice was left outside the League in 1919.

The Dumbarton Oaks proposals held out no hope of a millennium. This was not the kind of document that could stir after-dinner orators to eloquent speeches about eternal peace. And that was good. Too often during the past quarter of a century well-intentioned men and women had spoken piously of peace as if it were something that could be picked up at bargain counters; as if peace were something that did not have to be worked for, fought for, sacrificed for, as we are ready to work and fight and sacrifice for war. The Dumbarton Oaks proposals showed plainly that nations would have to make concrete undertakings and accept concrete responsibilities if they were to have any measure of peace and stability after the war.

The Dumbarton Oaks document had another great virtue. It made an effort to reconvert, for peacetime use, the machinery of collaboration that the United Nations had developed for purposes of war. The Military Staff Committee, to be composed of the Chiefs of Staff of the five great powers in the Security Council, was a continuation of an Allied agency that had proved very effective for the waging of the war. That agency was the Combined Chiefs of Staff in Washington, whose members mapped out the global strategy for Britain and the United States, in consultation with the Chiefs of Staff of Russia and China and, later, of France and the liberated nations of Europe. The Economic and Social Council, also, provided for a carry-over of wartime machinery, since under its general authority could be brought all the economic and social agencies developed by the United Nations that can be usefully continued into peacetime. This carry-over of experience is of great importance for the future expansion of international collaboration. During World War I the Allies had also developed joint machinery, but the moment the war was over the machinery created at so much cost in blood and treasure was scrapped. This time a definite attempt was being made to utilize the international "know-how" acquired during the war years.

The Dumbarton Oaks proposals, excellent as far as they went, were open to a number of criticisms and queries which were immediately raised by the small nations, and by public opinion in the United States and Britain. Among these the following deserve most attention, because they were subsequently discussed at length at the San Francisco conference.

Is Security Council a Great-Power Dictatorship?

Many people expressed the fear that the Security Council could easily become a dictatorship of the great powers. They pointed out that the great powers, by the very fact that the military resources of all the United Nations would be placed at the disposal of the Security Council, would be in a position to impose their dictates on the small nations. This danger certainly exists, although the six smaller nations who will be non-permanent members will have a voice in the decisions of the Council, and the Big Five will have to gain the votes of at least two of them for any decision. But even so it is true that the permanent members could, if they wanted, transform the Security Council into a Concert of the World, on the pattern of the Concert of Europe which the great continental powers established in 1814 after the defeat of Napoleon. This Concert kept the continent relatively at peace during the first half of the nineteenth century by checking every attempt at territorial change or revolution.

We have to face the fact, however, unpleasant as it may seem, that the Big Five control among them about 60 per cent of the population of the world, and a large part of the world's resources, industrial potential, and military power. They would be far more dangerous to the small nations if left to their own devices than if they are part of an international organization where they have obligations as well as privileges. There is no authority strong enough to stop the great powers if they choose to go on the rampage, singly or in concert. The great powers alone can curb each other, and when they begin to do that, they will be at war. In the final

analysis the only protection against misuse of power by the
Big Five is a sense of restraint and responsibility on their
part. This is what Russia meant when it tried to assure small
nations at San Francisco that the Big Five would not abuse
their veto power. But the need for such a sense of responsibility and restraint makes it particularly important that the
citizens of the United States, Britain and France, where
freedom of public discussion exists, should continuously urge
their governments to respect the rights of small nations.

Will Small Nations Have Too Little Authority?

Another criticism made of the Dumbarton Oaks document
was that it gave too little authority to the small nations. It is
true that the great powers assured themselves a privileged
position at Dumbarton Oaks. But there is no use pretending
that Venezuela has the influence in world affairs exercised
by the United States, or that Luxemburg is equal in power
to Britain, or Iran equal in power to Russia. In these still
barbaric days we measure the influence of a nation not by the
contribution it has made to human civilization—on that score
some small nations would rank ahead of some great powers
—but chiefly by its military and industrial strength. Meas-
ured by this yardstick, there is no question that there are
really only three great powers in the world after the defeat
of Germany and Japan—the United States, Britain, and Russia. China is ranked as a great power quite rightly, because of
the greatness of spirit of its four hundred million people;
but neither in military nor industrial terms is China comparable to the other three great powers among the United
Nations. France has exercised for centuries, and does again
today, a far-reaching moral and intellectual influence, and
thus can claim a place among the great powers; but in mod-

ern times this influence has been far in excess of France's military and industrial potential. It may well prove practicable, as suggested by Canada, to recognize an in-between category of nations—the "middle" powers. These would be countries like Canada which, because of their resources and technical skill, can make a larger contribution in military and industrial terms to the maintenance of international security than some of the nations called "small." Thus Canada, and other middle nations, could be asked to assume greater responsibilities for the maintenance of world security, and at the same time be granted greater authority in decisions about war and peace. But in the final analysis the responsibility for maintaining security will rest for some time to come with the United States, Britain, and Russia.

Will this mean the decline of the small nations, the destruction of their independence? Will they become mere slaves of the great powers? This could happen if the great powers show themselves irresponsibly ready to trample over any weak nation that seems to be in their way. But the prospect need not be as grim as some people paint it. True, all great powers, at some stage in their history, have committed unfair or cruel acts toward smaller or weaker peoples. Yet on occasion great powers have shown themselves capable of self-restraint. During World War II, in spite of many irritations and outright danger to British security, Britain scrupulously respected the neutrality of Eire. The United States, after establishing bases in Brazil for prosecution of the Battle of the Atlantic, is returning these bases to the Brazilians.

In the future, if the great powers really succeed in affording a measure of security to the small nations, the latter could then practice, without constant fear of war, the arts of peace in which many of them have proved peculiarly adept. The small nations may then find that they have exchanged what had become the mere shadow of national sovereignty for the substance of security against aggression—for surely a Poland that could be conquered by Germany in less than a month and a Denmark that could be overrun by the Germans in one day did not find safety in sovereignty. Moreover, we must remember that there will be six small nations on the Security Council, and that any type of majority vote would require concurrence by at least one of the small nations. Small states, too, will be expected to contribute military forces and facilities to the United Nations organization to the extent of their ability.

In working out relations between the great powers and the small nations we are facing the eternal problem involved in human relations: the problem of finding a practicable formula that will combine freedom and order. The small nations must have freedom to develop their own institutions, to speak their own language, to practice their own traditions. But this freedom can be enjoyed by all only if there is some orderly way of adjusting conflicts that arise from time to time—and arise not merely between great powers or between great powers and small, but also among the small nations themselves. Once such orderly machinery has been established, the small nations, which would have an equal voice with larger ones in the General Assembly and in the Economic and Social Council, could contribute out of their long experience to the settlement of the economic and social problems that some of them—notably the Netherlands, Norway, Denmark—have already courageously faced and adjusted at home.

What Will Happen to National Sovereignty?

Still another criticism of the Dumbarton Oaks document was that it failed to come to grips with the issue of national sovereignty which proved so great a stumbling block to effective action by the League of Nations. The United Nations, according to the document, was to be "based on the principle of the sovereign equality of all peace-loving states." Nothing in the proposals made it possible for the organization itself to limit the sovereign rights of member nations—except in the case of a threat to the peace or breach of the peace—unless the nations themselves were willing to accept such limitations. Clearly we are in a transitional stage of international development when nations realize that they will not achieve security solely by clinging to the absolute concept of national sovereignty, and yet are not ready to abandon, at least officially, their support of this concept.

The United States is just as jealous of its sovereignty as other nations. This is understandable, for all peoples have an emotional feeling about sovereignty which symbolizes the affections and loyalties they have for their countries. We cannot expect that this emotional attitude will be ended overnight by a document. Most American spokesmen are still fearful of saying anything that could be interpreted, at home, as a "sacrifice" of this nation's sovereignty. The idea dies hard that by collaborating with other nations we are bound always to "lose" or "sacrifice" something. It is difficult to convince people that through such collaboration we would also gain something, as we gained in time of war by receiving the aid all over the globe of people to whom we, in turn, extended assistance. One of the few leaders in this country who had the courage to tackle the sovereignty issue was Wendell Willkie when he said, shortly before his death: "Sovereignty is something to be used, not hoarded." His was a positive idea of sovereignty, not a negative one. Instead of saying that we cannot do this or that as a nation because such actions would in some way affect our sovereignty, we should say: "We, the American people, are sovereign, and we intend to use our sovereign powers to undertake this or that measure which seems best to serve the nation's interests at this time."

If our people come to the conclusion that collaboration with other nations for the achievement of security is in the national interest, then any measure we may take to attain that end will be an exercise of sovereignty, not an encroachment on it. But considerable time may pass before people in this country and in other nations develop such an attitude toward their relations with each other. The war itself has made a change in the concept of sovereignty more difficult, because it has sharpened the national consciousness of all peoples and has made them more jealous of their rights and independence. This, again, should not discourage us. For human institutions grow very slowly.

Why Not an International Police Force?

The question of sovereignty becomes particularly acute when we try to determine the use of force by the United Nations organization. On this score another criticism of the Dumbarton Oaks document was that it did not provide for a genuine international police force. This criticism is just if by international police force we mean a force recruited from citizens of all nations removed from the control of their own governments and responsible solely to the United Nations organization. Such a force is the ideal objective of those concerned with the building of an effective security system.

But for the time being at least, because of the prevailing desire to maintain national sovereignty, it is difficult to persuade any nation—least of all the United States—to place all or part of its armed forces exclusively under the control of the United Nations organization. The provisions of the Dumbarton Oaks document for the use of force by the United Nations organization represented a compromise between the views of those who insisted that a nation should use its armed forces only to protect itself, and those who urged that all national armed forces should be used only by an international organization for the protection of any nation that is a victim of aggression. Under the Dumbarton Oaks arrangement, every nation would retain control of its armed forces. Each, however, would sign a special agreement by which it would undertake to make available to the Security Council, on its call, specified "armed forces, facilities and assistance necessary for the purpose of maintaining international peace and security." It would thus be possible for the United States, for example, to maintain all our armed forces, except certain air force units, within our own borders. Then, when called on by the Security Council, we would dispatch our armed forces, in accordance with the terms of our special agreement, wherever they were needed to check aggression.

This, admittedly, is not an ideal arrangement, because it still leaves each nation free to decide what forces it will place at the disposal of the Security Council. But it is a step forward for nations to agree that some military force be available to the Council, and it does represent a voluntary limitation of national sovereignty. In practice, the arrangement would be similar to the pattern of military collaboration worked out by the United Nations during the war. On the western front, for example, American, Canadian, British, French and other forces, all retaining their national identity and their own officers, fought together under the command of an American, General Eisenhower. In the China-Burma-India theater of operations, American, British, Indian, Chinese, and other troops fought side by side under Admiral Lord Mountbatten, an Englishman. This same arrangement would apply to the air force contingents which, under the Dumbarton Oaks proposals, should be held immediately available to the Security Council for "combined international enforcement action." It might prove necessary, however, to effect closer integration of command in the case of the air force contingents, so that no time may be lost in using them in an emergency. Perhaps it would be necessary to base them at specially designated international bases at strategic points, from which they could most effectively enforce the decisions of the Council.

How Would Security Council Decide Use of Force?

The mere availability of national armed forces for use by the Security Council, however, will not of itself assure action by the Council, unless the representatives of the nations composing it have authority to act promptly when an emergency does arise. At this point too, the Dumbarton Oaks document was criticized on the ground that it had not sufficiently reduced the exercise of national sovereignty. If the Council is to act promptly, it will be necessary for every nation to give its delegate sufficient authority to vote for the use of military force without prolonged consultation with the home government that might hold up action. Otherwise, an aggressor nation would always have the initial advantage,

since, with the use of modern weapons like long-range bomb-
ers and robot bombs, an aggressor could conquer a small
nation long before an international council, whose members
had first to confer at length with their governments, could
possibly swing into action.

The measure of authority to be granted by each nation to
its representative on the Security Council has already occa-
sioned considerable debate in the United States. It will occasion more now that the United Nations Charter has
been ratified by the Senate. The manner in which the United
States decides to handle this question will indicate to other
nations the extent to which we are ready to back up an effective system of collective security. In the United States it is
Congress that decides on declaration of war; so if any action
for the enforcement of international security proposed by
the Security Council is regarded as an act of war, the American representative would have to wait for the decision of
Congress before he could cast a vote—and this might be a
matter of weeks or even months. By contrast, the decision
for Russia could be taken promptly by Stalin, the decision
for Britain by the British Cabinet, the decision for China
by Chiang Kai-shek.

Yet it is entirely natural that Congress should want to
retain control over actions of the United States that might
involve the use of American forces. How can this problem
be adjusted? Of course, it might be decided that international
action to check aggression is not the same thing as war between nations, and therefore does not require decision by
Congress. President Roosevelt, in his address of October 21,
1944, to the Foreign Policy Association in New York, suggested a different approach when he said that the American
representative on the Council "must be endowed in advance

by the people themselves, by constitutional means through their representatives in Congress, with authority to act." A somewhat similar statement was made by Governor Dewey in his reply to the President's foreign policy speech on October 24 in Minneapolis.

The President, as Commander-in-Chief, has power to employ the country's armed forces abroad for the protection of United States citizens and agencies. On a number of occasions American forces have been so used on the decision of the Executive, without prior consultation with Congress—notably for the suppression of pirates along the coasts of Africa, during the Boxer rebellion in China in 1900, and in various uprisings in Latin America. A different question will arise if American forces are to be used for the protection of the lives and property of other peoples. It would be dangerous, however, if Congress were to limit the use of our armed forces, as suggested by some, to the Western Hemisphere, where we happen to have strategic and economic interests. If each great power did the same thing and specifically provided where it would permit its forces to be used, the authority of the Security Council to act in an emergency would be gravely weakened, and probably destroyed. Nations would then tend to rely on regional rather than international arrangements for their security.

How Will Regional Arrangements Fit into World Organization?

The question of which comes first—regional or world security—was another moot point raised about the Dumbarton Oaks document. The document itself states that nothing in its terms "should preclude the existence of regional arrangements or agencies for dealing with matters relating to the maintenance of international peace and security as are appropriate for regional action, provided that such arrangements or agencies and their activities are consistent with the purposes and principles of the Organization." But it also provided that no enforcement action should be taken by regional agencies or under regional arrangements without the authorization of the Security Council.

In theory, there would seem to be no more incompatibility between regional arrangements and an international organization than there is between the municipal and state administrations and the federal government in this country. But in practice there is a great difference. For within our federal structure, local and state units, while autonomous in local and state matters, are subordinate to the federal administration in all matters affecting the nation as a whole. Such a system has not yet been worked out in international affairs. And until the United Nations organization has become firmly established, there will be constant danger that regional blocs, created by nations to safeguard their security, may claim powers equal, not subordinate, to the international organization. Regional combinations of small states constitute no danger to international organization; but neither do they offer security to their members. The Scandinavian bloc, the Little Entente, and the Balkan Federation were unable to withstand Germany before 1939. Regional blocs dominated by great powers can be strong. But regional blocs dominated by the great powers might well defy the decisions of the Security Council, and instead of wars between nations we might then come to have wars between regions or continents.

We thus face a vicious circle. For unless an international organization capable of assuring the security of all nations, large and small, is firmly established, nations in various geographic regions will tend to group themselves together for the purpose of achieving a modicum of security. Before the war was over the countries of Eastern Europe were already grouping themselves around Russia, and the Scandinavian and Low Countries around Britain, while the countries of Latin America drew closer for security purposes to the United States. Yet once regional blocs have been formed, the nations composing them may acquire certain vested interests in regionalism, and may be less ready to work with an international organization. The relationship of bilateral and regional security arrangements to a system of collective security came up in a sharp form at the San Francisco conference, as we shall see in Chapter IV.

Are There Any Prospects for World Federation?

For the time being, at least, there is no prospect of a closely knit world federation similar to the structure of the United States. Desirable as such a federation may seem, it is precluded by the vast differences in political, economic, and social development that exist among nations, by the divergences in their policies resulting from differences in historical experience, and by their mutual doubts and suspicions which, in many cases, have been enhanced rather than alleviated by the war. These doubts and suspicions can be removed and these differences can be leveled only by a slow process of working together, day in and day out, on problems of mutual concern. The United Nations organization would provide continuous opportunities for just such a process.

However, some people have thought that the creation of the United Nations organization would be facilitated if it were preceded by the creation of a European federation, and were disappointed by the absence of any federation proposals in the Dumbarton Oaks document. The idea of a European federation has appealed to many statesmen throughout the ages—in our own time particularly to the French Foreign Minister, Aristide Briand, who advocated a European Union. But some of the factors which today prevent the formation of a world federation work also against a European federation. Moreover, many of the European nations have interests that go far beyond the boundaries of the continent. France has her overseas empire and cultural ties with Latin America; the Netherlands has colonies in Asia; Belgium, Spain, and Portugal have colonies in Africa; and Sweden and Norway have a stake in world commerce. These countries have little desire to be confined to a continental federation.

Nor is there agreement as to which nations should be included in a European federation. Britain certainly has important strategic and economic interests in Europe, especially in the Low and Scandinavian countries, and in the lands bordering on the Mediterranean. But Britain can by no means be described as a European country, and its concern with overseas trade long ago transformed it into the kernel of a vast empire with ties all over the world. Russia occupies a strategic position in Europe, but Russia, too, is not an exclusively European country, for it occupies a comparably important position in Asia. If Britain and Russia, which are often regarded by Europeans as non-European countries, are excluded from a European federation, then that federation will inevitably come to be dominated by Germany, which is still the most powerful industrial nation on the continent, and the one possessing the largest and most technically skilled population. A federation so dominated by Germany could hardly offer any security to France or the smaller nations of Europe, and would be viewed with suspicion and fear by Britain and Russia, as well as by the United States.

One more thing should be borne in mind when discussing the relative advantages of federation within regions or continents, as compared with a world organization. The same technological developments—the airplane and the atomic bomb, the possibility of transporting millions of armed men across oceans for the invasion of one continent by another— that have made national units obsolete for purposes of security have made regions and continents similarly obsolete. It is often pointed out that countries like China and the states of Latin America have leaped without transition from the ox-drawn cart to the airplane, by-passing the age of railways. In a comparable sense the international community has jumped from the national unit to the practical fact of "one world," by-passing what under more leisurely circumstances might have been the stage of regional or continental federation.

Thus, the moment the Dumbarton Oaks proposals had been published and submitted for discussion by the small nations, and by the citizens of all the United Nations, it became apparent that the machinery they proposed could not be considered as if it were to function in a vacuum. This machinery had to be immediately related to the multifarious problems of world affairs it would ultimately have to settle. The next step was to discuss some of these problems, which was done at the Yalta conference.

CHAPTER II

THE YALTA CONFERENCE
February 4–12, 1945

THE conference held by President Roosevelt, Prime Minister Churchill and Marshal Stalin, accompanied by their respective advisers, at Yalta in the Crimea from February 4 to 12, 1945, was in the nature of a preliminary peace conference. It was only in part concerned with the problems of world organization discussed at Dumbarton Oaks. The steadfast purpose of President Roosevelt had been to keep the consideration of the machinery needed to assure international security separate from the negotiations regarding peace settlements in Europe and Asia. Many critics of the Paris Peace Conference had pointed out that the Allies undertook an insuperable task in 1919 when they tried at one and the same time to draw up the Covenant of the League of Nations and to decide a multitude of specific territorial and political issues raised by the various allied and associated powers while preparing the Treaty of Versailles. In the light of this experience, it had been thought advisable to discuss the terms of the Charter of the United Nations in an atmosphere undisturbed by the manifold conflicts that inevitably arise among the victors when the hour comes for negotiation of peace terms with the enemy.

Desirable as this objective unquestionably was, the rapid

unfolding of the Allied military campaigns in Europe during the months following the Dumbarton Oaks conference made it necessary to deal with certain territorial and political problems on the continent before the peace machinery of international organization had been established. As a result, several of Europe's most controversial issues, which preferably should have been submitted to a General Assembly or Security Council of the United Nations, were settled by the leaders of the United States, Britain and Russia at Yalta.

How Was Germany To Be Treated?

The problem that overshadowed all others in Europe in 1945, as the Allies invaded German soil, was the treatment to be accorded Germany. At the Yalta conference President Roosevelt, Prime Minister Churchill and Marshal Stalin declared that "Nazi Germany is doomed. The German people will only make the cost of their defeat heavier to themselves by attempting to continue a hopeless resistance." They announced that they had agreed on "common policies and plans for enforcing the unconditional surrender terms" which they planned to impose together on Germany after German armed resistance had been finally crushed. But they said that these terms would not be made known until the final defeat of Germany had been accomplished. They gave, however, a broad preview of their future intentions.

Germany, they declared, would be occupied by the three great powers, each of which was to control a separate zone. A central control commission composed of the supreme military commanders of the three powers, with headquarters in Berlin, would coordinate Allied administration. France would be invited to participate in this commission and to take over a zone of occupation, if she so desired.

The Big Three said that it was their inflexible purpose to destroy German militarism and Nazism and "to insure that Germany will never again be able to disturb the peace of the world." All German armed forces were to be disarmed and disbanded; the German General Staff was to be broken up "for all time"; all German military equipment was to be removed or destroyed; all German industry that could be used for military production was to be eliminated or controlled; all war criminals were to be brought to just and swift punishment; reparation in kind was to be exacted for the destruction wrought by the Germans; the Nazi party, Nazi laws, organizations and institutions would be wiped out; all Nazi and militarist influences would be removed from public office and from the cultural and economic life of the German people; and all other measures necessary to the future peace and safety of the world would be taken by the three great powers "in harmony." However, the three leaders declared that it was not their purpose to "destroy the people of Germany, but only when Nazism and militarism have been extirpated will there be hope for a decent life for Germans, and a place for them in the comity of nations."

With regard to the specific matter of reparation, it was "recognized as just that Germany be obliged to make compensation for . . . damage in kind to the greatest extent possible." A reparation commission was created, with headquarters in Moscow, which was to be instructed to consider the extent and methods for compensating damage caused by Germany to the Allied countries.

What Future for Liberated Europe?

The three leaders declared that they had agreed "to concert during the temporary period of instability in liberated Europe the policies of their three governments in assisting the peoples liberated from the domination of Nazi Germany and the peoples of the former Axis satellite states of Europe to solve by democratic means their pressing political and economic problems." They expressed the hope that France would become associated with the Big Three in their efforts to aid the stabilization of Europe.

The Yalta communiqué made clear the intention that such changes as might take place in Europe should be carried out in accordance with the Atlantic Charter and the Declaration of the United Nations which reaffirmed the charter. "The establishment of order in Europe and the rebuilding of national economic life," it was stated at Yalta, "must be achieved by processes which will enable the liberated peoples to destroy the last vestiges of nazism and fascism and to create democratic institutions of their own choice. This is a principle of the Atlantic Charter—the right of all peoples to choose the form of government under which they will live—the restoration of sovereign rights and self-government to those peoples who have been forcibly deprived of them by the aggressor nations."

To foster such conditions, the Big Three undertook jointly to assist the people in any European liberated state or former Axis satellite in Europe where, in their judgment, conditions required them to: (1) establish conditions of internal peace; (2) carry out emergency measures for the relief of distressed peoples; (3) form interim governmental authorities broadly representative of all democratic elements in the population, pledged to the earliest possible establishment, through free elections of governments responsive to the will of the people; and (4) to facilitate where necessary the holding of such elections. The three governments said they would consult the other United Nations and provisional authorities, or other governments in Europe, "when matters of direct interest to them are under consideration."

By these methods it was hoped to avert, in the future, such clashes as had occurred between the Big Three in 1944 over Russia's unilateral actions in Poland and Britain's unilateral actions in Greece. However the phrase "democratic means" was not defined, and shortly after Yalta differences arose once more when Russia took a hand in the political shakeup in Rumania. This brought to power the government of Premier Groza, to whom Stalin turned over the civilian administration of Transylvania, which was detached by Hungary from Rumania before 1939, but surrendered under Hungary's armistice with the United States, Britain and Russia. An even deeper conflict of views arose concerning the method of broadening the provisional government of Poland which had been established in Lublin on December 31, 1944, under the sponsorship of Moscow. This government was composed of Leftist elements little known outside Poland, and included Communists and Communist sympathizers. The Soviet government recognized the Lublin regime, later transferred to Warsaw, while the United States and Britain continued to recognize the Polish government in exile in London.

What Was Decided About Poland?

At Yalta the leaders of the Big Three declared that "a new situation had been created in Poland as a result of her complete liberation by the Red Army." This, they added, called for the establishment of a Polish Provisional Government "which can be more broadly based than was possible before the recent liberation of western Poland." It was therefore decided that the Lublin regime should "be reorganized on a broader democratic basis with the inclusion of democratic leaders from Poland itself and from Poles abroad." This broadened government was then to be called the Polish Provisional Government of National Unity.

To facilitate this change, V. M. Molotov, Soviet Foreign Commissar, W. Averell Harriman, American Ambassador to Moscow, and Sir Archibald Clark-Kerr, British Ambassador to Moscow, were authorized as a commission to consult in "the first instance" with members of the Lublin regime and with other Polish democratic leaders, from within Poland and from abroad, with a view to the proposed reorganization of the Lublin regime. The resulting Government of National Unity was to be pledged to the holding of free and unfettered elections as soon as possible on the basis of universal suffrage and secret ballot. In these elections all democratic and anti-Nazi parties were to have the right to take part and to nominate candidates.

The special commission designated for this task found it impossible to reach an agreement, reportedly because of Russia's objections to the Polish leaders abroad who had been suggested for inclusion in the broadened government. A difference of opinion also arose over interpretation of the Yalta agreement. The United States and Britain apparently understood that an entirely new government, composed of individuals drawn from the Lublin regime, from London, and from other groups in Poland, should be formed; while Russia's interpretation was that the existing Lublin regime should merely be broadened by the addition of new members. Having failed to reach an agreement, the four great powers sponsoring the San Francisco conference—the United States, Britain, Russia and China—did not include Poland among the countries invited to the conference. On March 22, however, the Soviet government requested in London and Washington that the Polish Provisional Government, which by that time had been transferred from Lublin to Warsaw, should be invited to attend. This request was turned down by both the United States and Britain.

Meanwhile, the leaders of the Big Three reached a decision about some of Poland's territorial problems. They came to the conclusion that the eastern frontier of Poland should follow the Curzon Line, which was proposed by Russia in January 1944, as the boundary between the two countries "with digressions from it in some regions of five to eight kilometers in favor of Poland." Again agreeing with proposals made by Russia, they recognized that Poland "must receive substantial accessions of territory in the north and west," at the expense of Germany. They stated, however, that the opinion of the new Polish Provisional Government of National Unity should be sought "in due course" on the extent of these accessions, and that the final delimitation of the western frontier of Poland "should thereafter await the peace conference." Without waiting for the peace conference, the Warsaw government raised the Polish flag over Danzig and adjacent areas at the end of March, as soon as these territories had been conquered by Russian armies.

What Was Done About Yugoslavia?

More successful in their immediate results were the decisions taken at Yalta about Yugoslavia, another liberated country which had threatened for a time to become a bone of contention between the Big Three. The conferees agreed to recommend to Marshal Tito, the Partisan leader, and Dr. Subasitch, Premier of the Yugoslav government in exile in London, that the agreement the two men had reached on November 1, 1944, which had been approved by King Peter under pressure from the British, should be put into effect immediately and that a new government should be formed on the basis of that agreement. The formation of this new government was announced in Belgrade by Marshal Tito and Dr. Subasitch on March 1, 1945. The conferees also recommended that, as soon as the new government had been formed, the anti-Fascist Assembly of National Liberation should be extended to include members of the last Yugoslav Parliament who had not compromised themselves by collaboration with the enemy, thus forming a body to be known as a temporary Parliament; and that legislative acts passed by the anti-Fascist Assembly of National Liberation would be subject to subsequent ratification by a Constituent Assembly. Thus it was hoped to legalize the measures taken by the Partisans during the war period. It was also announced, without further details, that there had been at Yalta a general review of other Balkan questions.

What Was Decided About International Organization?

The Big Three leaders undertook, at Yalta, to settle some of the questions left unanswered by the Dumbarton Oaks conference. They declared that they were "resolved upon the earliest possible establishment" with their allies of a general international organization to maintain peace and security. They expressed their belief that this was essential, both to prevent aggression and to remove the political, economic and social causes of war through the close and continuing collaboration of all peace-loving peoples. With this aim in view, they agreed that a conference of the United Nations should be called to meet at San Francisco on April 25, 1945, to prepare the charter of such an organization, along the lines proposed in the Dumbarton Oaks conversations.

The Yalta Voting Formula

The conferees also considered the question of voting procedure in the Security Council, which had been left open at Dumbarton Oaks. Announcement of the arrangement reached on this matter at Yalta was withheld until the Big Three had had an opportunity to consult with China and France, who were invited to sponsor with them the San Francisco conference. On March 5, Secretary of State Stettinius informed the Mexico City conference of the compromise worked out at Yalta. This was simultaneous with the issuance from Washington of invitations to San Francisco, which set forth the voting procedure in the Security Council. The Yalta formula distinguished between two types of matters on which the Security Council might vote: procedural matters, and "all other matters," sometimes described in subsequent interpretations as "substantive." On procedural matters such as adoption or alteration of rules of procedure, determination of method of selecting the Council president, selection of times and places of the Council's regular and special meetings, and so on—in other words questions involving the internal governance of the Council—decisions were to be made by an affirmative vote of any seven members, whether permanent or non-permanent, that is, by a simple majority. On all other matters decisions were to be made by an affirmative vote of seven members including the concurring votes of the permanent members. In other words, if, on a "substantive" matter one of the permanent members declined to vote, it could effectively prevent a decision.

This power of any one of the five permanent members to prevent a decision under these circumstances is what is known as the "veto power" of the Big Five. However, in all cases where the Council was discussing the peaceful settlement of a dispute, a state party to the dispute, even if one of the Big Five, was to abstain from voting. Only when the Council had to decide on action to be taken in the dispute could the permanent member who was party to the dispute veto the application of sanctions up to and including military force against it. As we shall see in Chapter V, the issue that arose at the San Francisco conference concerning the voting procedure of the Council was not the veto power of the Big Five, but the range of "substantive" matters over which it extended.

The League of Nations Covenant, it will be recalled, had provided that the League Council could reach decisions only by unanimous vote of all its members, permanent and non-permanent. This unanimity rule resulted in deadlocks on crucial questions. The Yalta formula provided for qualified unanimity—requiring unanimity only by the permanent members, who would then still need the votes of two non-permanent members to reach a decision on a "substantive" matter. Or, as it has been sometimes said, the Yalta formula provided for a "qualified" majority in the case of the permanent members.

The problem already discussed in the chapter on the Dumbarton Oaks proposals—how an international organization can place limitations on a great power—was thus only partly resolved at Yalta. However, the Yalta agreement marked a step forward over the Dumbarton Oaks conversations in the sense that at least it was agreed that a great power accused of threatening the peace would not have the right to prevent submission of the dispute for consideration by the Security Council. The procedure was clearly explained by Secretary of State Stettinius at Mexico City on March 5, when he said:

"This procedure means that whenever any member of the Council—including any permanent member—is a party to a dispute, that member cannot vote in any decision involving peaceful settlement of that dispute. Consequently, the Council can examine the dispute thoroughly and the remaining members can make recommendations to all the parties to the dispute as to methods and procedures for settling it. They can refer the legal aspects of the dispute to the international court for advice. They can refer the dispute to the General Assembly if they wish; and they can take any other appropriate steps short of enforcement measures to obtain a settlement of that dispute without the vote of the member of the Security Council involved in the dispute.

"This means that all members of the Security Council when they are parties to a dispute will be on the same footing before this Council. It means that no nation in the world will be denied the right to have a fair hearing of its case in the Security Council, and that the equal, democratic rights of all nations will be respected.

"If the dispute is not settled by such means, the major question before the Council is whether force needs to be employed. In that event, it is necessary that the vote of the permanent members of the Council be unanimous. They are the nations which possess in sufficient degree the industrial and military strength to prevent aggression. However, the decision of the Council can be reached in such a case only by a majority of seven members, which means that the permanent members cannot alone decide to take action. It also means that the nonpermanent members can prevent action."

It was hoped by some of the Yalta conferees that public discussion of disputes would encourage their settlement by methods short of war, before it had proved necessary to raise the question of the use of force by the Council when a great power accused of aggression could successfully block international action by voting against it. The method of voting, important though it is, is significant largely as a symbol of the willingness or unwillingness of nations to submit their disputes to peaceful arbitrament instead of the arbitrament of war. The more nations become accustomed to settling controversies that may arise between them by peaceful means, the less importance they will attribute to the procedure of voting.

The issue of votes, however, came up at the Yalta conference in another connection, not revealed in the official announcement published on February 12. It was only on March 29 that it was disclosed in Washington that Marshal Stalin had requested three votes in the General Assembly— one for the U.S.S.R., and one for each of two component republics, the Bielorussian * S.S.R. and the Ukrainian S.S.R. A statement from the White House said that President Roosevelt had agreed to the submission of Stalin's request to the San Francisco conference, but had said that if this request was acceded to, he in turn would ask for three

* Formerly known in English as White Russian S.S.R. "Biely" is the Russian word for white.

votes for the United States. On April 3, however, Secretary of State Stettinius declared that the United States would not press for three votes at San Francisco, although it would continue to support Russia's request.

The extent to which Stalin's demand for a vote for each of two of the component republics of the U.S.S.R. was influenced by internal Russian politics is a matter of speculation. The Ukrainian S.S.R., into which has been incorporated the Polish Ukraine, once part of Eastern Poland, has a long tradition of national consciousness. It may have been thought good politics in Moscow to give the Ukrainians as large a measure of outward autonomy as possible in the United Nations organization. Such considerations would not apply with equal strength in the case of the Bielorussian S.S.R. (which now includes Polish White Russia), where sentiments of national independence had never been as marked as in the Ukraine. It will be recalled that on February 1, 1944, Soviet Foreign Commissar Molotov had announced that each of the sixteen republics of the U.S.S.R. was henceforth to conduct its own foreign affairs and maintain its own military contingents. At that time it had been expected that the Soviet government—which had studied with interest the structure of the British Commonwealth of Nations and had come to the conclusion (not supported by the experience of the League of Nations), that all the Dominions invariably voted with Britain—would ask for sixteen votes in the United Nations organization. Thus Stalin's request for three votes at Yalta might have been regarded as a temporary modification of earlier, more far-reaching plans.

As long as the Security Council of the United Nations organization, however, is dominated in practice by the Big Three, it is difficult to see what, beyond prestige, is gained by additional votes in the General Assembly. It is obvious, moreover, that a great power can wield influence on the decisions of the General Assembly irrespective of the number of votes at its disposal. At the same time, several political scientists in this country have pointed out the incongruity of having equal numerical representation in the General Assembly for countries indubitably unequal in many respects, whether Luxembourg or Russia, Venezuela or the United States.

It has been suggested that votes should be accorded to different states on the basis of population (if this were done, China and India, not Russia and the United States, would have the largest number), taken together perhaps with such factors as economic development, social welfare, literacy, and so on. Under our federal system every state elects two Senators, but elects members of the House of Representatives on the basis of population. Some such system might eventually be introduced into the international organization. The question deserves dispassionate consideration. What is regrettable is not that it was discussed at Yalta, but that it was raised there in such a mechanistic form, with emphasis solely on an arbitrarily selected number of votes.

The Yalta communiqué, couched in blunt terms not calculated to arouse false optimism, stressed in closing that military victory and the establishment of the proposed international organization would provide "the greatest opportunity in all history to create in the years to come the essential conditions" of a secure and lasting peace. It gave no ground for the all too common belief that international machinery would of itself assure the security and general welfare of war-weary peoples. The task begun at Dumbarton Oaks remained to be completed at San Francisco and perfected at subsequent international gatherings.

CHAPTER III

THE MEXICO CITY CONFERENCE

February 21–March 8, 1945

THE Inter-American Conference on Problems of War and Peace, the first consultation of American Foreign Ministers in three eventful war years, met in Mexico City from February 21 to March 8, 1945. It was attended by all the nations who are members of the Pan American Union,* with the notable exception of Argentina. This conference was both a gathering to consider proposals for an international organization, and a preview of post-war problems in the Western Hemisphere. The twenty nations present discussed a wide range of subjects, including cooperative measures for the prosecution of the war; economic and social problems related to the transition period from war to peace and long-range improvements in the economy of the American nations; international organization for the maintenance of peace and collective security, as projected in the Dumbarton Oaks proposals; steps to strengthen the inter-American system and coordinate it with the United Nations organization; and the conditions—chief of which was declaration of war on the Axis powers—on which Argentina, whose government had been suspected of pro-Axis

* The Pan American Union, formed in 1890, is composed of the United States and the twenty Latin American republics.

leanings, would be readmitted to the Pan-American fold. The United States delegation, headed by Edward R. Stettinius, Jr., then Secretary of State, included two Senators— Warren Austin, Republican, of Vermont, and Tom Connally, Democrat, of Texas, and, as advisers, representatives of the A. F. of L. and the CIO.

Argentina Present Though Unseen

The main subject on the agenda, although not listed, was Argentina, just as Russia turned out to be the main unwritten subject on the agenda at San Francisco. Argentina, long a rival of the United States for leadership of the Latin American countries, had alone among these countries balked at breaking off relations with the Axis powers, and the Farrell "colonels'" government which had seized power in 1944 had increasingly displayed many of the characteristics of European Fascist and Nazi governments. The United States had declined to recognize the Farrell government, had enlisted the support of the rest of Latin America for its non-recognition policy, and had applied economic and financial pressure to Argentina.

Some of the Latin American countries disapproved of the methods of the Farrell government, and feared that the Argentine militarists would seek to encroach on the territories of neighboring states. Yet many Latin Americans were apprehensive that the pressure applied by the United States to bring about internal changes in Argentina might set a precedent for similar intervention in other countries of the Western Hemisphere, and expressed a measure of admiration for Argentina's determination to resist such intervention. At the same time pro-democratic elements in Latin America felt discouraged that the United States had not been more vigorous in supporting the pro-democratic and pro-Allied elements in Argentina at a moment when these might have successfully resisted the establishment of a military dictatorship. Thus two desires dominated the Mexico City conference so far as Argentina was concerned: to make Argentina as harmless as possible to its neighbors, by strengthening the inter-American system of security and enlisting the unqualified support of the United States for this system; and to bring Argentina back into the Pan-American family of nations, as a preliminary to including it in the United Nations organization—provided it fulfilled at least the minimum test for membership of the United Nations by declaring war on the Axis powers. The United States, which needed the support of the Latin American countries at the forthcoming San Francisco conference, was ready to meet them halfway with regard to Argentina, although there was considerable division of opinion both in the Washington Administration and in the United States delegations to Mexico City and San Francisco concerning the advisability of inviting an unmistakably Fascist government to join the United Nations organization. The situation was further complicated by the fact that Russia expressed open hostility to the Farrell government, which had shown itself intransigent toward Communism; while Britain, which has long maintained close economic and financial ties with Argentina, had only with great reluctance followed the United States in its policy of not recognizing Farrell, and welcomed the prospect of Argentina's return to the circle of reputable nations.

The Act of Chapultepec

The Mexico City conference adopted several important documents, notably the Economic Charter of the Americas and the Resolution on Reorganization, Consolidation and Strengthening of the Inter-American System (a system based on a series of treaties and agreements concluded during more than half a century by the United States and the twenty Latin American republics). But it is the Declaration on Reciprocal Assistance and American Solidarity, known as the Act of Chapultepec, which is of particular interest to students of plans for an international security organization. In this act the American nations reaffirmed certain fundamental principles which they had been incorporating into their international law since 1890 by means of conventions, resolutions, and declarations. Among these principles were the following:

The proscription of territorial conquest and the non-recognition of all acquisitions made by force;

The condemnation of intervention by a state in the internal or external affairs of another;

The recognition that every war or threat of war affects directly or indirectly all civilized peoples, and endangers the great principles of liberty and justice which constitute the American ideal and the standard of its international policy;

The procedure of mutual consultation in order to find means of peaceful cooperation in the event of war or threat of war between American countries;

The recognition that every act susceptible of disturbing the peace of America affects each and every one of them and justifies the initiation of the procedure of consultation;

The resolution that any difference or dispute between the American nations, whatever its origin, shall be settled by the methods of conciliation, or unrestricted arbitration, or through the operation of international justice;

The recognition that respect for the personality, sov-

ereignty, and independence of each American State constitutes the essence of international order sustained by continental solidarity, which historically has been expressed and
sustained by declarations and treaties in force;

The affirmation that respect for and the faithful observance of treaties constitutes the indispensable rule for the
development of peaceful relations between states, and treaties
can only be revised by agreement of the contracting parties;

That in case the peace, security or territorial integrity of
any American republic is threatened by acts of any nature
that may impair them, they proclaim their common concern
and their determination to make effective their solidarity,
coordinating their respective sovereign wills by means of the
procedure of consultation, using the measures which in each
case the circumstances may make advisable;

That any attempt on the part of a non-American State
against the integrity or inviolability of the territory, the
sovereignty, or the political independence of an American
State shall be considered as an act of aggression against all
the American states.

What Acts of Aggression Were Covered?

One of the most notable features of the Act of Chapultepec was the statement that "the security and solidarity of
the Continent are affected to the same extent by an act of
aggression against any of the American States by a non-
American State, as by an American State against one or more
American States." This provision is similar in character to
the Monroe Doctrine, unilaterally proclaimed by the United
States in 1820 with the object of preventing encroachments
by any non-American state on the Western Hemisphere. Its
significance lies in the fact that a policy once regarded as

specifically that of the United States was endorsed by all the American nations. At the same time, this provision envisaged the possibility of attack by an American state (Argentina was the unnamed potential aggressor) on one or more of its neighbors, and provided for the adoption of collective measures of security by all the nations of the continent against such an attack.

The nations represented at Mexico City declared that in case acts of aggression occurred, or there was reason to believe that an act of aggression was being prepared by any other state against the integrity and inviolability of territory, or against the sovereignty or political independence of an American state, they would consult among themselves in order to agree upon measures that it might be advisable to take. The delegates of some of the American nations, notably Colombia, Brazil, and Uruguay, had come to Mexico City with the intention of concluding binding agreements of a much more specific character, directed at a potential aggressor either outside or within the Western Hemisphere, and providing not merely for consultation but for collective action against the aggressor state. However, the United States delegates were not prepared to go so far, for two main reasons. First, they were reluctant to submit an undertaking of such far-reaching character to the Senate before that body had had an opportunity to consider the Charter of the United Nations organization that was still to be drawn up at San Francisco. Second, some of the United States delegates were not certain whether the proposals for collective action by the nations of the Western Hemisphere might not jeopardize the projected world organization and foster the creation of regional arrangements in other parts of the world—notably in Eastern Europe, where Russia had already concluded a mutual assistance pact with Czechoslovakia and was considering similar pacts with Poland and Yugoslavia, or in Western Europe, where both Britain and France had concluded alliances with Russia.

What Was the Security Formula Adopted?

On the advice of Senators Warren Austin and Tom Connally, members of the United States delegation, a compromise formula was finally worked out and embodied in the Act of Chapultepec. According to this formula, the signatory states recognize during the war that threats and acts of aggression against any one of their number, whether from within or outside the Western Hemisphere, "constitute an interference with the war effort of the United Nations, calling for such procedures, within the scope of their constitutional powers of a general nature and for war, as may be found necessary." These procedures were to include measures against aggression listed in the Dumbarton Oaks proposals, notably the recall of chiefs of diplomatic missions; breaking of diplomatic relations; breaking of postal, telegraphic, telephonic, radio-telephonic relations; interruption of economic, commercial and financial relations; and, finally, use of armed force to prevent or repel aggression. As far as the United States is concerned, this compromise formula enables the President to invoke wartime emergency powers already granted to him by Congress, without asking for special approval by the Senate.

It was provided that the principles and procedures of the Act of Chapultepec should become effective immediately, "inasmuch as any act of aggression or threat of aggression during the present state of war interferes with the war effort of the United Nations to obtain victory." This was another veiled reference to Argentina. Looking beyond the war, however, the Mexico City conference recommended that, for the purpose of meeting threats or acts of aggression against any American Republic following the establishment of peace, the American nations should consider the conclusion, in accordance with their constitutional processes, of a permanent treaty establishing procedures by which such threats or acts might be met. Such a treaty, when concluded, would have to be submitted, in the case of the United States, for approval by the Senate.

The Act of Chapultepec is regarded by some observers as in the direct line of succession to earlier proposals of a similar nature, notably Woodrow Wilson's plan to establish an American "League of States." It goes far in the direction of abandoning the principle repeatedly stated at previous Inter-American conferences that in the Western Hemisphere no state has the right to intervene in the internal or external affairs of another. In recent years, however, the American Republics had gradually come to adopt a concept of mutual defense, from the consultative principle laid down at the Buenos Aires Peace Conference of 1936 to the Havana Declaration of 1940 directed against a non-American aggressor. In the Act of Chapultepec the American nations proclaim their determination to maintain their solidarity against any threat or act of aggression against any one of them, from whatever quarter it may come.

Is Inter-American Arrangement Compatible with World System?

The act frankly states in its concluding section that it provides for a regional arrangement to deal with matters relating to the maintenance of international peace and security as are appropriate for regional action in the Western Hemisphere. However, it declares that the arrangements, activities and procedures it sets forth "shall be consistent with the purposes and principles of the general international organization, when established." Yet the moment the act was signed doubts were expressed, especially in the United States, whether the regional measures of security it outlined would, in practice, be compatible with the Charter of the United Nations organization. What would happen, it was asked, if the American nations decided to take steps against a threat or act of aggression which would not be approved by the Security Council? Or, conversely, what would happen if the Security Council decided to take action against an aggressor in the Western Hemisphere and met with opposition on the part of one or more of the American nations? Would Latin American nations be ready to take military action in the event of an act of aggression in some other continent?

The adjustment of possible divergences between the Inter-American system of security and the world security system, outlined in the Dumbarton Oaks proposals, was left by the Mexico City conferees to the San Francisco conference. In Resolution XXX, the American nations endorsed the Dumbarton Oaks proposals as a basis for future world organization. They felt, however, that this document left much to be desired in the way of adequate guarantees and stronger representation for the small nations. They had conveyed their views to the United States before the Mexico City parley in individual consultations with Secretary of State Stettinius in Washington and, subsequently, in official statements.

What Were Latin American Objections to the Dumbarton Oaks Proposals?

The various objections raised by the Latin American nations were coordinated by Foreign Minister Parra-Perez of Venezuela in a sixty-page document which set forth suggestions for the following changes and additions to the Charter of the proposed United Nations organization, which resemble in many respects the suggestions made by small nations in other continents.

1. The proposed world organization should have as its purpose the maintenance of peace and security to the end that the essential liberties of human beings are respected. It should not (according to Uruguay) require of its component states a certain form of government, but simply good faith and compliance with international obligations.

2. The organization should be based on the fundamental principle of the juridical equality of states, and all members should abstain from intervention in the internal or external affairs of another state.

3. All those sovereign nations disposed to observe the purposes and principles of the organization should be included in the membership.

4. The General Assembly should have powers to deal with any question affecting the peace and security of the world, and to examine any problem brought to it by the governments or the Security Council, and make recommendations on it. Any question requiring action should be referred to the Security Council by the General Assembly which, however, reserves the right to review the decision taken.

5. The Assembly should be empowered to admit new members on its own initiative, or by recommendation of the Council, and to suspend any member of the organization against whom the Council shall have taken preventive or enforcement action.

6. The Security Council's membership should be increased. In view of Latin America's contribution to the cause of the United Nations, these states should have greater representation in the council. Panama, Brazil, Paraguay, and Uruguay proposed that one Latin American country receive a permanent seat. Cuba and Chile

specified merely that the group of nonpermanent members be enlarged. Ecuador, Guatemala, Honduras, and the Dominican Republic suggested that the Assembly always elect three nonpermanent
members from among the Latin American nations, their selection
to be governed by alphabetical order. The "Mexican plan," sec-
onded by Colombia, proposed that the Council should be composed
of one representative for twelve members of the organization. Six
council members, designated "semi-permanent," would be those
states among them one Latin American country, whose responsibility for the maintenance of peace is heaviest by reason of their
power. They would be elected by the Assembly at eight-year intervals. The Assembly, in addition, would elect six states as temporary
Council members, among which two Latin American countries
should always figure. These countries would serve for two-year
terms.

7. The Security Council should have primary responsibility for the
maintenance of peace and security, and the members of the organization should obligate themselves to carry out the decisions of the
council. In a joint statement, Chile and Peru proposed, however,
that in the event a conflict arose outside this hemisphere, which
affects another continent or region and does not constitute a threat
to world peace, the American states should not be obliged to participate in operations of a military character.

The Latin American nations did not expect that all their
suggestions would be accepted at San Francisco and incorporated into the Charter of the United Nations organization.
They did not press for detailed consideration at Mexico
City, being more interested in the acceptance by the United
States of the regional security arrangements envisaged in
the Act of Chapultepec. They consequently agreed to support a resolution proposed by Mexico to the effect that the
Secretary of the Conference forward the views and suggestions of the American Republics to San Francisco where, it
was hoped, the United Nations would take them into consideration in drawing up the world charter. The resolution

made special reference to certain points on which "a consensus exists among the American republics represented in this conference that did not participate in the Dumbarton Oaks conversations." These points included the desire for universality of membership; the desirability of broadening and making more specific the enumeration of principles and purposes of the United Nations organization, as well as the powers of the General Assembly; the need to harmonize the powers of the Security Council with such changes in the powers of the General Assembly; the desirability of solving controversies of an inter-American character in accordance with inter-American methods, and of giving adequate representation to Latin America in the Security Council.

Although the United States was a party to this resolution, it was not clear to what extent this country concurred in its conclusions. The resolution did not commit this country to support these proposals at San Francisco, or to do more than take notice of them. While the Latin American countries thus had an opportunity to publicize their views on the Dumbarton Oaks proposals, action on their suggestions was deferred to the San Francisco conference.

The procedures for dealing with threats or acts of aggression in the Western Hemisphere were given substance by the Resolution on Reorganization, Consolidation and Strengthening of the Inter-American System, proposed by the United States. This clearly indicated that the United States had no intention of abandoning the Inter-American system in favor of the world organization, as had been feared by some of the American Republics. Probably the most important innovation suggested by the resolution was that the Pan American Union, in addition to its present duties, shall take action on every matter that affects "the effective functioning of the inter-American system and the solidarity and general welfare of the American Republics." This wording was generally interpreted to mean that the Union would receive powers to consult on political matters.

To avert the possibility, which had previously disturbed the American nations, that the United States would dominate the Pan American Union, the resolution provided for rotation of the chairmanship of its Governing Board (held in the past by the Secretary of State of the United States). At Mexico's suggestion, it also stated that members of the Board should not be Ambassadors accredited to Washington as in the past, but *ad hoc* delegates designated by each of the American Republics who would not be influenced in favor of the United States by their diplomatic connections. Secretary of State Stettinius declared at a press conference on February 23 that these changes in the Pan American Union were designed not only to make the Union more effective, but also to correlate its activities with the "broader program of world security."

Finally, in a closing session, the Mexico City conference adopted a resolution which deplored the fact that the "Argentine Nation" had not yet found it possible to take the steps that would have permitted its participation in the conference, and formally expressed the hope that it would adhere to the resolutions drawn up at that meeting, as well as orient its foreign policy in such a fashion as to "achieve its incorporation into the United Nations." The resolution asked, in effect, that to obtain diplomatic recognition Argentina adhere to the Act of Chapultepec and declare war on the Axis powers, but did not require Buenos Aires to undertake any internal political reforms. The Argentine government on March 27 declared the existence of a state of war with Japan and Germany—"in view of the character of the latter as an ally of Japan." The Pan American Union Governing Board unanimously approved a motion to open the Final Act of the Mexico City conference to Argentine adhesion on April 4; and on April 9 the United States, with other American countries, Britain, France, and others recognized the military government of Farrell after more than a year of diplomatic non-intercourse. The question of Argentina's admission to the ranks of the United Nations was destined to provide one of the most stormy moments of the San Francisco conference.

CHAPTER IV

THE SAN FRANCISCO CONFERENCE
April 25 to June 26, 1945

A Conference on Two Planes

THE United Nations Conference on International Organization, known as UNCIO, was held at San Francisco from April 25 to June 26, 1945, by 50 United Nations which had declared war on either Germany or Japan or both. They had met to draft a charter on the basis of the Dumbarton Oaks proposals of October 9, 1944.* This conference had a two-fold character. It was a gathering of technical experts whose task was to draft the constitution of a world organization. At the same time, it was a meeting of political leaders of countries in five continents whose thoughts, especially after V-E Day, were inevitably focused on the problems of the approaching peace settlement.

The conference thus functioned from the outset on two

* The following 50 nations were represented at the San Francisco conference: Argentina, Australia, Belgium, Bolivia, Brazil, Bielorussian S.S.R., Canada, Chile, China, Colombia, Costa Rica, Cuba, Czechoslovakia, Denmark, Dominican Republic, Ecuador, Egypt, El Salvador, Ethiopia, France, Greece, Guatemala, Haiti, Honduras, India, Iran, Iraq, the Lebanon, Liberia, Luxemburg, Mexico, Netherlands, New Zealand, Nicaragua, Norway, Panama, Paraguay, Peru, Philippine Commonwealth, Saudi Arabia, Syria, Turkey, Ukrainian S.S.R., Union of South Africa, U.S.S.R., United Kingdom, United States, Uruguay, Venezuela, Yugoslavia.

planes. There was an earnest determination to concentrate on the building of international machinery and to avoid discussion of specific political and economic issues, such as Russia's intentions in Europe and Asia, the treatment of Germany, the disposition to be made of territories taken from enemy states, the future of colonies, the connection between regional and collective security. These dominated the thoughts of all delegates both in committee meetings closed to the press, and in private conversations about post-war arrangements which gained in scope and intensity as the technical work of the conference drew to a close. Under the circumstances, the choice of San Francisco, from whose hills and wharves every visitor could see ships loaded with troops and materials departing for the Pacific theater of war and others returning homeward with victims of that war, proved to be an inspiration. For otherwise the political leaders and technical experts gathered at the conference might have been tempted to forget the urgencies of war and to become bogged down in conflicts about the peace.

Political Overtones

The intermingling of the political with the technical was strikingly illustrated in the early days of the conference. The conflict over the admission of Argentina revealed the determination of the United States and the Latin American countries to restore the solidarity of the Western Hemisphere, even at the risk of seeming to appease a Fascist government in Buenos Aires, and of alienating Russia, on whose behalf Foreign Commissar Molotov had urged that the decision should not be reached as if "rushing to a fire." The arrest of the sixteen Polish leaders who were subsequently placed on trial in Moscow cast a threatening shadow over the otherwise harmonious negotiations of the Big Four during the first week concerning amendments of the Dumbarton Oaks proposals. Political issues came to the fore again in the later days of the conference, when the delegations of Syria and the Lebanon, backed by the other members present of the Arab League * formed in Cairo in March 1945, vigorously opposed the dispatch of French reinforcements to the Levant—an incident that caused tension between France and the Arabs, as well as between France and Britain. And, while the conference opened with what many regarded as an unduly conciliatory gesture to Argentine Fascism, it closed with the acceptance of a proposal introduced by Mexico for the exclusion from the United Nations organization of any nation whose government had been aided by the Axis—an unmistakable reference to the Franco regime in Spain.

The political overtones and implications of the conference would make fascinating reading if they were ever to become known in full. This is extremely doubtful, if only because the personal likes and dislikes, the unspoken prejudices, and the emotional strains that shape human decisions can never be adequately reported even by those who have intimately participated in negotiations. But some trends of thought and action were sufficiently clear to be noted with a measure of certainty.

Critical Attitude Toward Russia

The most notable of these trends, and the one that threatened for a time to create the greatest difficulties in San Francisco, as well as in the capitals of Europe, was the critical

* The states members of the Arab League are Egypt, Iraq, Saudi Arabia, Syria, the Lebanon, Transjordan and Yemen. The first five were represented at the San Francisco conference.

attitude at first adopted toward Russia. The problem of Russia's future relations with the other 47 nations was the outstanding subject of discussion in and out of conference rooms, as if it had been written in, with invisible ink, throughout the otherwise scrupulously technical agenda. It had been assumed that the major issues between the Big Three had been ironed out at Yalta in February. But the San Francisco conference opened two months later in an atmosphere of renewed suspicion concerning Russia's aspirations in Europe and Asia. For this the ending of war in Europe was partly responsible. The defeat of Germany caused many people whose anti-Russian sentiments had been held in leash during the war to feel that, since Russia's military aid was no longer needed, the time had come to set limits to the expansion of Russian influence on the European continent or, as was often remarked in San Francisco, to "stiffen" Allied policy toward Russia.

The demand for a stiffer policy was strengthened by the deadlock reached in Moscow in carrying out the Yalta decision about the formation of a new Polish government. This deadlock had led some officials previously friendly to Russia to despair of ever reaching an agreement with the Kremlin. The Russians, for their part, did little to ease the strain that had developed between them and their Western allies. In the early days of the conference they continued to take unilateral actions in Europe, as when they recognized the Renner government in Austria without previous consultation with the United States and Britain, and announced the arrest of sixteen Poles, among whom were emissaries of the Polish government in exile sent to negotiate with Russia. Meanwhile, the possibility that, with the termination of hostilities in Europe, Russia, who on April 5 had denounced its non-aggression pact with Japan, might decide to take an active part in the Asiatic war, began to weigh on the minds of some of the delegates who feared that Russia would claim territorial rewards in Asia at China's expense.

Yet as the conference proceeded the give-and-take of daily negotiations did a great deal to alleviate the mutual fears and suspicions that had beclouded the opening sessions. The Western nations came to understand better than they had in the past the urgent reality of Russia's preoccupation with security against the renewal of German aggression. The Russians, for their part, were able to observe at close range how their abrupt unilateral actions affect other peoples— even those most eager for friendship with the U.S.S.R., and became gradually convinced that other countries are determined to build an effective system of collective security with, and not against it, as frequently suspected in Moscow.

How the Big Four Differ on Security

Much of the initial tension between Russia and the other great powers was due to differences of views concerning the nature of world security, which the UNCIO had been summoned to assure. President Truman, in his speech opening the conference, as in his address to Congress on April 16, 1945, stressed the responsibility of great powers not to use force except in defense of law. Great powers, he emphasized, must serve, not dominate, small nations. They must be "good neighbors." On behalf of China, which became a spokesman for the small nations in their demand for peace based on justice—not merely peace—Chinese Foreign Minister T. V. Soong pleaded for the creation of order based on respect for law. British Foreign Secretary Eden, who probably expressed best of all the sentiments of his listeners, declared that the great powers can make a twofold contribution: by supporting international organization; and by setting up standards of international conduct and observing them in relations with other nations. By contrast, M. Molotov stressed the effective authority of the international organization rather than its responsibility. He dwelt on the incapacity of the League of Nations to prevent World War II, and on the need for giving the new organization adequate military force that could be used promptly against an aggressor. Arguments about the rights of small nations or sovereign equality of all peoples, he said, should not become pretexts to weaken the machinery outlined at Dumbarton Oaks. In one of his press conferences he reiterated Russia's strong conviction that the great powers which have borne the burdens of war should be the ones to steer the world in the post-war period. Russia's emphasis on the need for effective military action, to be supplied primarily by the great powers, explains her insistence on a strict interpretation of the Big Five veto in the Security Council.

Two More Votes for the U.S.S.R.

The Russians were fully aware of the cooling off noticeable in Washington and London, as well as in San Francisco, and were particularly impressed by the solid front presented by the United States and the Latin American countries when M. Molotov, on April 30, requested a brief delay to consider the proposal for the admission of Argentina. As the Russians saw it, the Latin American countries, with 20 votes, if aligned with the United States, the Philippines and Liberia, plus the five Arab states which, having just created a regional unit, showed a lively interest in the Pan American Union, would always command a majority in the General

Assembly. This majority, in the opinion of the Russians, would hardly be favorable to the U.S.S.R. Although the Latin Americans vigorously declared that they would by no means always vote as a bloc, Russia's assumption does not seem to be wholly unjustified, in view of the anti-Communist sentiment, based on fear of social change, displayed in some Latin American circles. It was with this majority in mind that the Russians, at Yalta, had asked votes for Bielorussia (White Russia) and the Ukraine, two component republics of the Union of Soviet Socialist Republics. These two votes, granted at the opening of the San Francisco conference, may be regarded as a minimum demand, since the Soviet government, on February 1, 1944, had given all the sixteen republics composing the U.S.S.R. the right to raise their own armed forces and administer their own foreign policy. In answer to a question at a press conference M. Manuilsky, chairman of the Ukrainian delegation, unequivocally stated that the U.S.S.R. would eventually ask for sixteen votes. It may be noted, in this connection, that many of the Latin Americans opposed the grant of the two votes requested by Molotov; and acquiesced in the decision of the conference at the request of the United States only because it was made clear to them after Mexico City, that, in return, the United States would vote for the admission of Argentina.

Predominance of Non-Europeans

The early alignment of the Latin American countries against Russia underlined another notable trend at the San Francisco conference—and that was the predominant role played by non-European countries. At the close of a grueling six years' war, in which the countries of Europe had suffered grievous losses of men and materials, the Europeans found that the center of gravity had shifted from their continent to three great extra-European powers—the United States, Britain and Russia, which had borne the brunt of the war effort. This could have been anticipated, and accepted with more or less good grace. What was more striking, and from the European point of view more disturbing, was that the San Francisco conference was dominated, numerically, by the Latin American countries which, with a few minor exceptions, had contributed little to the fighting in Europe, and had benefited considerably by Allied purchases of their strategic raw materials and the development of some of their natural resources, notably rubber. Similarly, the Arab states, which had been strategically valuable to the Allies but had not actively participated in the war and, indeed, had gained by the Allies' urgent need for their oil resources, sometimes played a part out of proportion to their war effort.

Meanwhile Europe, bled white by war, Nazi terrorism, and Nazi economic depredations, seemed relegated to the background. Only the Netherlands, Belgium, Luxemburg, Norway, Czechoslovakia, Yugoslavia, Greece and Turkey were there to represent the small nations of Europe—with Denmark invited to join them in the final stages at the urgent request of Norway. Sweden, Switzerland, Spain, Portugal, and Eire were absent because they had not declared war on the Axis. Finland, Hungary, Rumania, Bulgaria and Italy were absent because they had fought on the Axis side. Poland was not invited because the Big Three had been unable to agree on the composition of its government.

France, still in the throes of recovering the confidence and prestige it had lost in the debacle of 1940, seemed at first to waver between championship of the small nations against the Big Four and return to the role of a great power. It was clear from the beginning, however, that what France wanted to obtain in the peace settlement—control of the Rhineland, international administration of the Ruhr, and return of Indo-China—could be achieved only with the aid of the great powers; and Foreign Minister Georges Bidault succeeded in having France admitted to the ranks of the Big Five, and seated as a permanent member of the Security Council forthwith and not "in due course," as provided in the Dumbarton Oaks proposals. Czechoslovakia, liberated by Russian and American forces during the early stages of the conference; Yugoslavia, where the government of Marshal Tito felt greatly indebted to Russia; and on occasion Norway, which regarded the behavior of the Russians in its northern region as "correct," tended to vote with Russia. Greece, too, although regarded by Russia within the British sphere of influence, under the leadership of its Leftist Foreign Minister, John Sofianopoulos, supported some of Russia's proposals.

Old World Seems New

In spite of their small number, the inevitable difficulties of representing countries which had not yet had an opportunity to choose their governments in free elections, and the problems of human and material reconstruction in their homelands, the Europeans, as time went on, gained increasing influence at the conference. The moderation of Foreign Minister Spaak of Belgium, which reflected well the constructive middle-of-the-road attitude of the Belgian delegation; the diplomatic skill of Sofianopoulos; the hopeful spirit of the Norwegians; the outspokenness of the Netherlands Foreign Minister, Van Kleffens; the intellectual clarity of the French—all contributed to the success of the negotiations.

The European delegations gave non-Europeans a foretaste of the new forces stirring on the continent. This was particularly true of the French delegation, which contained many members of the resistance movement, beginning with Foreign Minister Georges Bidault. The Europeans were like convalescents from a grave illness. They had lived through the Nazi plague and, having survived, were henceforth invulnerable to its poison; while countries which had been physically untouched by war and Nazi terrorism seemed in some respects susceptible to infection. The New World, as represented by the Latin Americans, sounded often old, and potentially or actually reactionary, when compared with the Old World of Europe.

The British, too, in spite of their great sufferings and sacrifices, appeared frequently unaware of the ferment on the European continent and in the colonial world. In contrast not only to their European neighbors, but also to the Dominions, the British expressed views still strongly influenced by nineteenth century concepts of diplomacy and imperialism. Britain, whose economic strength had been seriously undermined by the war, and whose strategic position had been jeopardized by the development of air power, was forced to play out of weakness at the conference. But even under these unfavorable circumstances it retained, at the conference, a position of world leadership.

No Anglo-Dominion Bloc

The many contrasts, and even conflicts, that emerged between the views of Britain and those of its Dominions (contrasts and conflicts even more strongly expressed at the British Commonwealth conference that preceded San Francisco) definitely dispelled the myth of an Anglo-Dominion bloc which, as a matter of record, had never existed in the League of Nations. Australia, under the vigorous and sometimes blustering leadership of Dr. Herbert Vere Evatt, Attorney General and Minister for External Affairs, who expressed the kind of suspicions about diplomatic intrigues that used to be voiced in the American press, and New Zealand, under the leadership of its equally determined but more adaptable Prime Minister, Peter Fraser, opposed Britain on a wide range of subjects, notably trusteeships, and repeatedly questioned the British interpretation of the Yalta voting formula. Canada, represented as usual by an able and devoted group of officials, showed little interest in trusteeships, but made an outstanding contribution in its carefully thought-out proposals for expansion of the functions and authority of the Economic and Social Council. India's principal delegate, Sir Ramaswami Mudaliar, distinguished himself as chairman of the Committee on Economic and Social Cooperation by his skill in reconciling conflicting points of view and his forward-looking spirit.

Role of United States

The delegation of the United States, after a period of tension when it had to wrestle with the question of Argentina's admission and seemed to be aligning itself with Britain against Russia, notably on the Polish question, assumed the role of a mediator. This role it tactfully used to steer the conference between the extremes of great-power authoritarianism, advocated by Russia, and domination of the proposed international organization by the numerically superior small nations, who demanded equality of rights with the great powers without being able to accept equality and responsibility. The presence in the delegation of Senators Vandenberg and Connally was of the highest tactical value. Not only did their advice permit the delegation to avoid pitfalls which might otherwise have prevented acceptance of the Charter by the Senate, but the two Senators' intimate knowledge of the negotiations made them persuasive advocates of the document when it was presented to the Senate for ratification.

Secretary of State Stettinius did not possess so great a knowledge of international affairs as some of his predecessors in that office, and lacked experience in that field; but his dynamic energy, his determination to carry the conference through to a successful conclusion, and above all his genuine desire to see a workable document accepted by the participating nations contributed to the success of a difficult undertaking that might have disheartened one less buoyant.

Commander Harold E. Stassen and Senator Vandenberg emerged as the leading personalities in the delegation. Commander Stassen had not only taken unusual pains to inform himself beforehand concerning the subject matter of the conference, but impressed fellow-delegates by his lucid understanding of the issues at stake and his tactful skill in negotiations, notably on the controversial subject of trusteeships. Senator Vandenberg labored incessantly to include in the Charter the American concepts of justice, law, and peaceful change, and did everything in his power to make the Charter a document that could not fail to be ratified by the Senate.

Initiative Left to Russia

It would have been helpful if the United States and Britain had, at the outset, assumed stronger leadership of the conference, and formulated in terms that could stir popular imagination the objectives for which they thought the war had been fought and peace machinery was being established. Their failure to assume such leadership left the initiative for a time in the hands of M. Molotov, who effectively availed himself of the opportunity, especially at his three lively conferences with the press. In the course of the last one, held on the eve of his return to Moscow, the Foreign Commissar placed Russia in the vanguard of nations demanding protection of human rights (among which he listed the right to work, with a broad hint at the prospect of post-war unemployment) and measures to advance the welfare and independence of colonial peoples. No one can possibly claim that citizens of the U.S.S.R. do not enjoy all the rights and privileges advocated by Molotov for other nations. Nevertheless the contrast between the reluctance or inability of the Western powers to define their aims in Europe and Asia, and Russia's forthrightness both in formulating and pursuing its objectives, created serious problems in San Francisco and in Allied councils and will persist even when the machinery of international organization has been established, until the Big Three find a common ground for their policies.

Charter Not Ideal

The most encouraging aspect of the conference was that, in spite of profound divergences among fifty nations differing widely in historical development, political traditions, and economic and social systems, it proved possible, after nine weeks of intensive work, to reach agreement on a Charter of the United Nations organization. This Charter, being a man-made document, is not ideal. But it represents a remarkably wide area of agreement on highly controversial issues. And it is wiser to build modestly within the limits of the practicable than to fail grandiosely by seeking the unattainable.

The Charter should not be regarded with cynicism or discouragement. For it is a genuine attempt to liberalize the Dumbarton Oaks proposals, drawn up by the Big Four and inevitably, for that reason, reflecting the great powers' concept of the post-war world. The very fact that forty-five middle and small nations (France having joined the ranks of the Big Five) were afforded ample opportunity to discuss, criticize, and amend the Dumbarton Oaks proposals is a step forward from unchallenged great-power authoritarianism, and offers hope that, as the world gains a feeling of security, further liberalization may be achieved through eventual amendment of the Charter. Those who regard the League of Nations as more democratic than the United Nations organization should recall that the League Covenant was drafted by the Big Five of 1919—the United States, Britain, France, Italy and Japan—and put into operation without any prior consultation with smaller nations.

Historians will never be able to bring against the San Francisco conference the famous accusation brought against the Congress of Vienna of 1815: "Le Congrès danse, mais n'avance pas." This was a hard-working conference. The delegates of fifty nations grouped into four main Commissions—General Provisions, General Assembly, Security Council, and Judicial Organization—subdivided in turn into twelve committees, labored literally day and night to produce, in the light of the bitter experience of the past quarter of a century, a system of collective security that could not only check aggression once it had begun but, far more important, could alleviate the causes of conflicts among nations. They took the Dumbarton Oaks proposals as their working draft and, in the course of their labors, covered with flesh and articulated at many joints a scheme of international organization which the proposals had presented in skeleton form.

Core of Dumbarton Oaks Kept

The core of the Dumbarton Oaks proposals is retained essentially unaltered in the Charter. This core is the coalition of the great powers, victors in World War II, who assume responsibility for the maintenance of world security and claim authority sufficient to discharge this responsibility. The great-power coalition is embedded in the structure of the Security Council. For the time being, at least, and presumably until the obligation to prevent a nation's resort to war has become an accepted routine matter for all nations, the coalition will be the central organ of the United Nations Organization, known for short as UNO.

As provided in the Dumbarton Oaks proposals, the Security Council is to be composed of one representative of each of eleven members of the organization, of which five—the United States, Britain, Russia, France and China—are to have permanent seats. The other six members are to be elected by the General Assembly. The efforts of some delegations at San Francisco to enlarge the membership of the Council were defeated. In deference, however, to the wishes of a number of middle and small nations, notably Canada and Australia, the Charter provides that, in electing the six non-permanent members, "due regard" is to be "specially paid, in the first instance to the contribution of members of the United Nations to the maintenance of international peace and security and to the other purposes of the organization, and also to equitable geographical distribution." As provided at Dumbarton Oaks, the Security Council—unlike the League Council which was to "meet from time to time as occasion may require"—is to be so organized "as to be able to function continuously," and each state member of the Security Council shall for this purpose be represented at all times at the seat of the organization. The continuous operation of the Council and the limited number of its members should insure close cooperation between national representatives in that body. The same thing is true of the Military Staff Committee, which is also to sit continuously.

Use of Force Strengthened

The enforcement machinery of the Security Council has been further strengthened in the Charter as compared with the Dumbarton Oaks document. The special agreements whereby member nations are to specify "the armed forces, assistance and facilities" they are to place at the disposal of the organization, which originally were to have been concluded "among themselves," thus entailing considerable delay and possibly inconclusive negotiations, are now to be "negotiated as soon as possible" on the initiative of the Security Council and concluded "between the Security Council and members or between the Security Council and groups of members."

To the "facilities" granted by member states have been added in the Charter, at the suggestion of France, "rights of passage necessary for the purpose of maintaining international peace and security." It is in this connection that one should read the new membership requirements set forth in Chapter II, paragraph 4, of the Charter which declares that membership in the organization (once the original members have been mentioned), is open to "all other peace-loving states" which, in the judgment of the organization, are able and willing to carry out the obligations of membership. In other words a state, no matter how peace-loving, which is not ready to give the United Nations organization the armed assistance and facilities necessary to carry out a member's obligations under the Charter, would be unable to become a member. This provision, also urged by France, would exclude countries determined to preserve their neutrality, for example, Switzerland. Should Switzerland or other neutral countries eventually decide to seek membership in the United Nations organization, this provision of the Charter would in effect mean the end of neutrality. The Charter, like the Dumbarton Oaks document (and in contrast to the League Covenant, which provided for eventual disarmament) emphasizes not disarmament, but effective international security enforcement measures, to be followed by stabilization and regulation of national armaments. Unlike the Dumbarton Oaks document, it gives states which are not members of the Security Council but are called on to place armed forces at the Council's disposal, an opportunity to be heard before force is used on the principle of "no taxation without representation." Article 44 provides that, when the Security Council has decided to use force it shall, before calling upon a member state not represented on it to provide armed forces, invite that member, if the member so desires, to participate in the decisions of the Security Council concerning use of that state's armed forces.

Controversy over Veto Power

One of the tensest moments of the conference came when Russia insisted that the Big Five should have the right to veto not only investigation of any dispute and decision to take enforcement action with respect to it, but also its discussion at any stage. The view expressed by Russia aroused alarm and vigorous opposition among other delegations, including those of the United States and Britain. To understand the controversy which for a few days appeared to threaten the success of the conference, it must be recalled that the Dumbarton Oaks proposals had made no provision concerning the voting procedure in the Security Council, merely stating that this question was "still under consideration." At the Yalta conference of February 1945, President Roosevelt, Prime Minister Churchill and Marshal Stalin agreed on a formula which was announced by the United States government on March 5. The Yalta formula, given in Chapter II of this book, was proposed by President Roosevelt himself. His main purpose was to maintain responsible unanimity among the only powers that could conceivably back up decisions of the Security Council with force. The veto power was thus not merely negative in conception. It was based on the positive assumption that no action to preserve or restore peace could probably be successful unless the Big Five agreed upon it unanimously.

Since the minutes of the Yalta conference are not available to the public, it is difficult to say with any assurance whether the United States, Britain and Russia clearly agreed at that time in their understanding of the matters that would come within the scope of the veto power. There seems to be no doubt that all of the Big Three intended to retain a veto over any decision to take enforcement action, on the ground that, since they would have to supply the bulk of the military and industrial forces in enforcement action against an aggressor, they had to have the right to decide whether or not to take such action. Although the middle and small nations would have preferred to see the permanent members of the Security Council abandon their veto power over enforcement action, they conceded that the Big Five had reasons for adopting the position they did on this issue. What the "little 45," under the unflagging leadership of Dr. Evatt of Australia, fought for was to remove all other matters from the scope of the Big Five veto. They were especially determined to see to it that the Big Five would be unable to exercise a veto over discussion of any dispute, regarding this as the heart of the democratic process and over amendments to the Charter, regarding this restriction as essential to their acceptance of a document which is admittedly imperfect, but which could in later years be perfected by the process of amendment.

Differences between Big Three

From the point of view of Russia, the Security Council was an instrument to carry out the decisions of the Big Five, not an organ for discussion. The decisions of the Big Five would presumably continue to be taken through diplomatic channels, or at special conferences such as those held at Moscow, Teheran, and Yalta. The Russian delegates, therefore, insisted on the need for unanimity of the Big Five on all issues—the kind of unanimity which, admittedly, had been essential for the prosecution of the war; and, at the same time, urged fellow-delegates to trust the great powers who, they contended, would not abuse the veto power and would use it sparingly.

The United States and Britain, for their part, took the view that all members of the Security Council should be free to discuss any dispute threatening the maintenance of international peace and security. Only at the point where the Security Council was called upon to take action of any kind— from a decision to investigate the dispute to a decision to adopt enforcement measures against an aggressor—should the veto power of the permanent members go into effect. In distinguishing between discussion of a dispute and a decision to investigate it, the United States contended that, beginning at this point, decisions and actions by the Security Council could have major political consequences and might initiate a "causal chain" of events which might, in the end, require the Council to invoke measures of enforcement.

It should be pointed out—because this matter has been widely misunderstood—that the United States was just as determined as Russia to retain a veto over enforcement. In fact, some members of the American delegation stated that, without such a veto the Charter would not obtain Senate ratification. British Foreign Secretary Eden, at a press conference held on the eve of his return to London, indicated that Britain was ready to be more liberal than either the United States or Russia, and was ready to remove the veto from investigation. It is possible that Mr. Eden took this position to placate the representatives of the Dominions, who vigorously questioned the veto power, and repeatedly queried Sir Alexander Cadogan, who had acted on behalf of Britain in the drafting of the Yalta formula. Whatever may have been the reason for Mr. Eden's statement, it was subsequently whittled down to a considerable extent by official interpretations of other members of the British delegation. In any case the United States and Britain agreed that the democratic right of free discussion insisted upon by the middle and small nations should be preserved so far as possible without impairing the efficacy of the Security Council in safeguarding world security.

Stalin's Concession on Veto

Following prolonged negotiations in San Francisco and a direct appeal to Marshal Stalin through Harry Hopkins, on a special mission to Moscow for the purpose of settling the controversy over the composition of the Polish regime, it was announced on June 7 that Stalin had instructed the Russian delegation to abandon its request for a veto over discussion of international disputes and to show a "conciliatory" attitude in "the interests of the success of the conference." The next day the Big Five announced an agreement clarifying the Yalta formula. According to this statement, unanimity of the permanent members of the Security Council is required in all decisions relating to enforcement action and, except as to parties to disputes (who must abstain from voting), in all decisions for peaceful settlement. The unanimity requirement, however, does not apply to the right of any nation to bring a dispute before the Security Council, and "no individual member of the Council can alone prevent consideration and discussion by the Council of a dispute or situation" thus brought to its attention. Once this clarification had been made, and twenty-two questions asked by the "little 45" had been answered by the Big Five on June 8, the Yalta formula was embodied in the Charter as Article 27.

One of the principal criticisms made of the Dumbarton Oaks proposals holds true of the San Francisco Charter: and that is that any one of the great powers, by the exercise of the veto over enforcement action, can prevent the Security Council from acting against it—or anyone else. In other words, the Security Council, as now organized, is geared to prevent wars between small nations, but not to prevent wars in which any one of its permanent great power members is involved. This is true. But it is also true, as has been repeatedly pointed out in the course of discussions about the Charter of the United Nations organization, that if things have reached a pass where some of the great powers have to take enforcement action against others, that in itself will be a state of war. The only safeguard against such a situation is not any particular piece of machinery, but the development of a sense of self-restraint and responsibility on the part of the great powers sufficient to prevent them from taking actions that might lead to war.

A more fundamental difficulty is that the builders of the United Nations organization had in mind the prevention of aggression by the nations that have been aggressors in World War II—specifically Germany and Japan. If the aggressor of the future should again be Germany or Japan, then the Security Council, embodying the victorious coalition of the Big Five, is well constructed to meet that eventuality. It is only if war should come from some other quarter that the question whether the Security Council is adequate to prevent it will be sharply posed.

"Humanization" of Dumbarton Oaks

While leaving the Security Council essentially as it was intended to be under the Dumbarton Oaks proposals, with the added authority to recommend terms of settlement of a dispute, and even strengthening its enforcement authority, the Charter "humanizes" and liberalizes the proposals in five important respects. It broadens the objectives of the United Nations organization; expands the powers of the General Assembly; enhances the position and enlarges the functions of the Economic and Social Council; extends the jurisdiction of the organization by establishing an international trusteeship system for dependent peoples to be administered by a Trusteeship Council; and seeks to integrate bilateral and regional security arrangements into a system of collective security.

Justice and Welfare Stressed

The Dumbarton Oaks proposals, framed by representatives of the Big Four when the global war was at fever pitch, understandably placed chief emphasis on the collective use of military force to prevent future acts of aggression. The danger of this approach, unless accompanied by measures to prevent war, was that peace might become synonymous with order imposed by force, with little or no consideration for justice and human welfare. This danger was promptly recognized by the small nations and by public opinion in Britain and the United States; and the Dumbarton Oaks document was criticized by many on the ground that it was in essence a hard-boiled military security arrangement, containing no reference to the undying hopes of mankind for a better world. At San Francisco these hopes were embodied in the preamble to the Charter (the Dumbarton Oaks proposals had no preamble), whose preparation was entrusted to a committee headed by Marshal Smuts, Premier of the Union of South Africa, sole survivor of the leading statesmen who had drafted the League of Nations Covenant in 1919.

The preamble, the work of many hands, as finally adopted, lists matters that had been left out of the Dumbarton Oaks proposals—human rights, the dignity and worth of the human person, justice and respect for obligations arising from treaties and other sources of international law, and the promotion of social progress and better standards of living in "larger freedom." To achieve these ends the member nations undertake "to practice tolerance and live together in peace with one another as good neighbors"; to unite their strength to maintain international peace and security; to insure "that armed force shall not be used, save in the common interest"; and "to employ international machinery for the promotion of the economic and social advancement of all peoples." This preamble reflects the concern of many delegates, and of the fighting and suffering men and women they represented, that the human values cruelly and systematically debased by the Nazis and Fascists should become the cornerstones of the new organization.

In similar vein Chapter I of the Charter, on the purposes and principles of the organization, enlarges considerably on the corresponding chapter of Dumbarton Oaks. It emphasizes the achievement not merely of peace, but of peace "in conformity with the principles of justice and international law." Friendly relations among nations are to be not relations imposed, however benevolently, by the great powers on their small neighbors, but to be based "on respect for the principle of equal rights and self-determination of peoples." International cooperation is to cover not only the solution of political, economic and social problems, but cultural problems as well, the term "cultural" being understood to include education. Among newly listed purposes of the organization are also "promotion and encouragement of respect for human rights and for fundamental freedoms for all without distinction as to race, sex, language, or religion."

Mere Words—or Deeds?

Skeptics may dismiss the preamble and the new phrasing of the chapter on purposes and principles of the organization as so many fine, but empty, words. It is obvious, of course, that if the member nations do not have the will to apply the principles they claim to support, the Charter will remain a dead letter. To the skeptics it seemed that the signing of the Charter had not altered the policies of nations by one iota. They could point out that, barely had the ink dried on the official texts of the Charter (drawn up in English, French, Russian, Chinese and Spanish), than Russia obtained from Czechoslovakia the cession of Ruthenia whose people were given no opportunity to exercise "self-determination," and asked Turkey for bases in the vicinity of the Straits of Dardanelles in a manner that the Turks regarded as not consonant with "the principle of equal rights."

It would be certainly unrealistic to overlook these great-power manifestations. At the same time, we must realize that it will take a long time for nations to learn how to practice what they preach. During the transition period when the United Nations organization gradually becomes established, and gains sufficient strength and influence to safeguard the security of all its members, some nations—especially the great powers—will be tempted and again and again fall back on the lonehand way of seeking to achieve security. This almost primitive urge of nations to take up diplomatic or military cudgels for their own defense against threats, real or fancied, is a vestigial remnant in international relations, as the appendix is in the human body. Only as time goes on, and nations become accustomed to the use of collective action, can we hope that this vestigial remnant will gradually disappear.

In this connection, it is encouraging that determined pressure to "humanize" the Charter was brought to bear on the United States delegation by consultants representing forty-two national organizations which had been invited by the State Department to present the views of their constituents. This experiment in establishing a link between public official opinion and officials representing the people at an international conference proved so successful that it should be repeated at future gatherings—and enlarged to include public opinion representatives of the other United Nations. For in the long run governments representing member nations in the organization will be guided by what they believe to be the desires and aspirations of their peoples, who thus have the ultimate power to determine the character and effectiveness of the United Nations organization. Even dictatorships are sensitive to popular sentiment. But if the United Nations organization is to function effectively the nations composing it must enjoy freedom to discuss political, economic and social problems at home, as well as freedom to communicate their views to other nations.

General Assembly as World Forum

One of the major achievements of the middle and small nations in their unremitting efforts to liberalize the Dumbarton Oaks proposals was the transformation of the General Assembly, originally slated for a rubber-stamp role, into a world forum for discussion of "any questions or any matters within the scope of the present Charter." This formula, proposed by Dr. Evatt of Australia, was adopted on June 20 after Russia had expressed apprehension that the General Assembly, which in an earlier draft had been granted the broad right "to discuss any matter within the sphere of international relations," might proceed to discuss affairs that member nations regarded as internal in character. It should be noted that one of the main principles of the organization is that nothing in the Charter "shall authorize the United Nations to intervene in matters which are essentially within the domestic jurisdiction of any state."

In contrast to the League of Nations, where there was duplication of powers at many points between the Assembly and the Council, the General Assembly is to have functions distinct from those of the Security Council. "The General Assembly may discuss any questions relating to the maintenance of international peace and security brought before it by any member of the United Nations, or by the Security Council, or by a state which is not a member of the United Nations"; and "may make recommendations with regard to such questions to the state or states concerned or to the Security Council, or both. Any question on which action is necessary shall be referred to the Security Council by the General Assembly, either before or after discussion." The General Assembly also has the right (which it did not have under the Dumbarton Oaks proposals) to call the attention of the Security Council "to situations which are likely to endanger international peace and security." But, as provided at Dumbarton Oaks, while the Security Council "is exercising in respect of any dispute or situation the functions assigned to it" in the Charter, the General Assembly shall not make any recommendation unless the Security Council so requests.

The most important change in the status of the General

Assembly effected by the Charter is the provision it makes for close and continuous cooperation between the Assembly and the Security Council. Under the Dumbarton Oaks proposals the Security Council could have functioned as an authoritarian, independent organ, dominated by the Big Five, with no responsibility to the Assembly. The Charter, by contrast, provides that the Secretary-General of the organization, with the consent of the Security Council, shall notify the General Assembly at each session * of any matters relative to the maintenance of international peace or security which are being dealt with by the Security Council and shall similarly notify the General Assembly, or the members of the United Nations if the General Assembly is not in session, immediately the Security Council ceases to deal with such matters.

Article 15 of the Charter also provides that the "General Assembly shall receive and consider annual and special reports from the Security Council; these reports shall include an account of the measures that the Security Council has decided upon or taken to maintain international peace." These provisions are designed not only to establish the responsibility of the Security Council to the Assembly, but also to prevent the possibility that the Council might pigeonhole matters threatening international peace and security, blocking further action on these matters by the Assembly. The General Assembly is a deliberative, not a legislative body. But it will be able to keep a close and continuous check on the activities of the Security Council, as a legislature in democratic countries keeps check on the activities of the executive. It will also have the right to reopen

* The General Assembly is to meet annually, while the Security Council, as mentioned above, is to sit in continuous session.

discussion of matters affecting international peace and security the moment the Council, having failed to act, ceases
to deal with such matters.

In harmony with the "humanization" of the objectives
and purposes of the organization, the Charter provides that
the General Assembly shall initiate studies and make recommendations for the purpose of promoting international cooperation in cultural, educational, and health fields, in addition to the political, economic, and social fields specified in
the Dumbarton Oaks document. It is also to assist "in the
realization of human rights and fundamental freedoms for
all, without distinction as to race, sex, language or religion,"
and to encourage "the progressive development of international law and its codification." The General Assembly,
moreover, is to recommend measures for "the peaceful adjustment of any situation, regardless of origin, which it
deems likely to impair the general welfare or friendly relations among nations, including situations resulting from a
violation" of the purposes and principles set forth in the
Charter.

Here, again, the provisions of the Charter could remain
a dead letter if the nations should prove apathetic about
using the General Assembly as their sounding board, and exercising their right to inquire into and comment upon the
activities of the Security Council. The lively debates over the
veto power, over regionalism versus collective security, over
trusteeships, which marked the San Francisco negotiations,
however, are a hopeful portent of the scope of discussion
that may be expected to develop in the General Assembly
once the United Nations organization gets into its stride.
But for this purpose, too, it is essential that the representatives of member nations should feel free to engage in frank

and open debate, and not be limited in the expression of opinion by fear of being disowned or reproved by dictatorial governments at home. The Assembly could, as often stated, become an international "town meeting." The most characteristic feature of a New England town meeting, however, is that all participants are at liberty to speak their mind—and speak it without fear or favor. This condition is yet to be attained in international relations.

Economic and Social Council Strengthened

The democratization and strengthening of the General Assembly go hand in hand with the expansion in status and functions of the Economic and Social Council. This Council had been originally included in the Dumbarton Oaks document as a sort of appendage to the General Assembly. It is still to act "under the authority" of the Assembly, but in the Charter it has become one of "the principal organs" of the United Nations organization, listed along with the Security Council, the General Assembly, the Secretariat, and the International Court of Justice. This change is particularly important because the Economic and Social Council, as provided at Dumbarton Oaks, is to be composed of eighteen members elected by the General Assembly without reference to whether they are great or small powers. In this respect it is a more democratic organ than the Security Council and, once the problem of assuring security by military force becomes less acute, could emerge as the outstanding agency of the organization, in which all nations, irrespective of their industrial and military potential, could contribute their best thought and effort to the prevention of war through the peaceful adjustment of economic and social problems. In this Council, the economic and social interests of nations could become so "mixed up" (to use Churchill's phrase about Britain and the United States) as to create a permanent, practical basis for collaboration in the sphere of politics.

The Charter gives a more detailed list than the Dumbarton Oaks proposals of the economic and social objectives the organization is to pursue "with a view to the creation of conditions of stability and well-being which are necessary for peaceful and friendly relations among nations based on respect for the principle of equal rights and self-determination of peoples." Among these objectives are higher standards of living, full employment, and conditions of economic and social progress and development; solutions of international economic, social, health and other related problems; and universal respect for and observance of human rights and fundamental freedoms for all without distinction as to race, sex, language, or religion.

Responsibility for the pursuit of these objectives is vested in the General Assembly and, under its authority, in the Economic and Social Council, whose scope has been broadened in accordance with a number of proposals submitted at San Francisco, the most interesting and elaborate of which was prepared by Canada. The Council is now empowered not only to carry out the recommendations of the General Assembly and to make recommendations on its own initiative, but also to make and initiate studies and reports with respect to problems coming within its competence, and to make recommendations, on its own initiative, on such matters to the General Assembly, to member nations, and to specialized organizations or agencies concerned. It may also arrange to obtain regular reports from specialized organizations or agencies and from member nations on steps taken to give effect to its own recommendations and to those of the

General Assembly, and communicate its observations on such reports to the Assembly.

In addition to the commissions in the economic and social fields provided for by the Dumbarton Oaks proposals, the Council is to set up a commission for the promotion of human rights, which will have the task of giving effect to the principles set forth in the preamble and statement of purposes of the Charter. The Economic and Social Council will thus be able to exercise general supervision over all international matters and activities within the broad fields of human endeavor assigned to it. According to the Charter, however, the organization has no jurisdiction over matters regarded by states as domestic in character. True, it has powers of recommendation only, and will have to act through technical agencies like the International Food and Agriculture Organization, UNRRA, the International Bank proposed under the Bretton Woods agreements, and others that may be brought "into relationship" with the United Nations organization. But if the United Nations so desire, this Council could become a powerful instrument for dealing with the multifarious economic and social problems which the war has left in its wake. These problems cut across boundary lines and require more than national action; if not alleviated, they will bear within them the seeds of another war.

Trusteeship for Dependent Peoples

The Charter contains an entirely new section on trusteeship for dependent peoples—a subject not mentioned in the Dumbarton Oaks proposals. President Roosevelt had been profoundly concerned with the problems of dependent peoples and trusteeship matters, and had taken to Yalta certain recommendations on these subjects. At Yalta Presi-

dent Roosevelt, Prime Minister Churchill and Marshal
Stalin agreed that the five permanent members of the Security Council should consult each other before the San
Francisco conference on providing machinery in the Charter
for dealing with territorial trusteeships, and that no discussions of specific territories were to take place during these
preliminary consultations or at San Francisco. It was to be
a matter for subsequent agreement as to which territories
within the three categories considered at Yalta (and subsequently included in the Charter) would actually be placed
under trusteeship.

The United States proposals on trusteeship submitted to
the UNCIO represented a compromise between the
views of the Navy and War Departments, which asked for
outright annexation of Pacific islands conquered by the
United States, and the views of the State Department,
which sought to establish a general principle to be observed
by all nations in the administration of dependent peoples.
The United States draft sought to distinguish between strategic and non-strategic areas. This distinction had an obvious
application to the Pacific islands, which for the most part
have few or no inhabitants, and therefore do not raise the
usual problems of Western rule over native peoples. By contrast, the trusteeship proposals submitted by Britain, while
containing no reference to the eventual independence of
colonies, stressed the responsibility of colonial powers for the
welfare and security of the peoples inhabiting territories
under their administration, whether strategic or non-strategic.

The cardinal feature of the three chapters (XI, XII and
XIII) devoted to dependent peoples is Chapter XI, entitled
Declaration Regarding Non-Self-Governing Territories.
This chapter (Article 73) declares that states which have re-

sponsibilities for the administration of territories whose peoples "have not yet attained a full measure of self-government" recognize the principle that "the interests of the inhabitants of these territories are paramount, and accept as a sacred trust [the phrase used in the League Covenant] the obligation to promote to the utmost, within the system of international peace and security established by the present Charter, the well-being of the inhabitants of these territories." To this end member states undertake to insure, "with due respect for the culture of the peoples concerned," their political, economic, social, and educational advancement, their just treatment and their protection against abuses; to develop self-government, to take due account of the political aspirations of the peoples, and to assist them in the progressive development of their free political institutions, "according to the particular circumstances of each territory and its peoples and their varying stages of advancement"; to further international peace and security; and to promote constructive measures of development. They also undertake to transmit regularly to the Secretary-General of the United Nations organization for information purposes (subject to such limitations as security and constitutional considerations may require), statistical and other information of a technical nature relating to economic, social, and educational conditions in the territories for which they are responsible. Under this declaration of general principles, applicable to all territories administered by colonial powers, the United States could accept the obligation to submit reports of statistical and other information of a technical nature on Puerto Rico, Hawaii and Alaska (which it publishes periodically) to the Secretary-General of the United Nations organization. This, however, was not the interpretation placed on the provision by the United States delegation.

Colonies and American Public Opinion

American public opinion, which has frequently expressed itself in favor of eventual independence for colonial peoples, may be disappointed by the failure of the San Francisco conference to come to grips with the problem of colonies. It would have been impossible, however, to have thrown the complex subject of colonial reform into the conference without thorough preliminary negotiations between the powers concerned, for which there had been no adequate opportunity before San Francisco. Moreover, it is not always clearly understood by Americans that colonial possessions are not idle luxuries or whims, but important factors of political, economic and strategic power for the Western nations that control them (as the Philippine Islands are for the United States). It is therefore unrealistic to expect these nations to surrender their possessions without adequate compensation in some other form, especially at the end of a war in which they are on the winning side. Nor do Americans always fully appreciate the fact that colonies differ widely in their political, economic and human problems; that no single formula can encompass the future of, let us say, Portuguese Timor and French Indo-China; and that the abrupt grant of independence without adequate preparation and provision for a minimum of political freedom, economic stability and military security might impair, rather than improve, the condition of dependent peoples.

The Charter's declaration of general principles concerning non-self-governing peoples is acceptable to colonial powers like Britain, France, the Netherlands and Belgium precisely because it is general, and entails no changes in the status of their colonies other than those they are willing to undertake on their own initiative. But the United States, by presenting its own territorial demands at the conference in proposals obviously, although not explicitly, applicable to the Pacific islands it claims on grounds of security, has weakened its right to urge other nations in the future to surrender control over territories which they, too, can claim are needed to safeguard their security.

What Is the Trusteeship System?

In addition to this declaration of general principles, the Charter provides for the establishment of an international trusteeship system for the administration and supervision of such territories, to be known as trust territories, as may be placed thereunder by subsequent individual agreements. The basic objectives of the trusteeship system are "to promote the political, economic, social and educational advancement of the inhabitants of the trust territories, and their progressive development toward self-government or independence as may be appropriate to the particular circumstances of each territory and its peoples and the freely expressed wishes of the peoples concerned, and as may be provided by the terms of each trusteeship agreement." The trusteeship system is also to encourage respect for human rights and for fundamental freedoms, in accordance with the preamble and purposes of the Charter, and to insure equal treatment in social, economic, and commercial matters for all members of the United Nations and their nationals, and also equal treatment for the latter in the administration of justice.

The use of the phrases "self-government" and "independence" aroused considerable controversy among the delegates.

Russia and China favored the use of the phrase "independence" for all dependent peoples, whether placed under the trusteeship system or not, while Britain, supported by the United States, favored the phrase "self-government" (in spite of the fact that it had promised independence to the Philippines by 1946). It was finally agreed to use only "self-government" in the general declaration on non-self-governing territories; and to provide for the alternative of self-government or independence, whichever seemed most appropriate under the circumstances, in the chapter on trust territories. As an illustration of its plans for colonial areas, Britain, during the conference, announced its intention to grant self-government to Burma as soon as practical circumstances permitted. The British also declared that they favored the extension to other colonial areas of the system of regional collaboration and supervision developed by the Anglo-American Caribbean Commission.

What Territories Will Come under Trusteeship?

The trusteeship chapter lists three categories of territories which may be placed in trust by means of special trusteeship agreements. These are: 1. Territories now held under mandate (this would include the only remaining Class A mandate, Palestine, a former Turkish territory held by Britain; Class B mandates over former German territories in Africa held by Britain, France, Belgium and the Union of South Africa; and Class C mandates over erstwhile German islands in the Pacific formerly held by Japan, and over German islands in that area held by Australia and New Zealand). 2. Territories which may be detached from enemy states as a result of the war (this would include Japanese-owned, as distinguished from Japanese-mandated, islands in the Pacific

—for example, Okinawa, and Italy's colonies in Africa).
3. Territories voluntarily placed under the system by states
responsible for their administration (this would include any
area now controlled by colonial powers).

The trusteeship arrangement for each territory to be
placed in trust is to be agreed upon by the states directly
concerned, including the mandatory power in the case of
territories now held under mandate by one of the United
Nations. This provision has been described as a "joker." For
countries which at subsequent peace conferences receive territories detached from enemy states (e.g. the United States
when it receives Japanese-mandated or Japanese-owned islands) are thus free to abstain from placing them under the
trusteeship system if they so desire. In this respect the trusteeship system falls short of the League of Nations mandates system, for in 1919 former German and Turkish territories were transferred directly to the League, which then
assigned mandates over them to various allied and associated
powers.

The Charter provides that, until trusteeship agreements
have been concluded, nothing in its terms "shall be construed
in or of itself to alter in any manner the rights whatsoever
of any states or any peoples or the terms of existing international instruments to which members of the United Nations
may respectively be parties." This provision was adopted to
prevent any possible change in the status of inhabitants of
League mandates, notably in Palestine, where states members of the Arab League had sought to make changes re-
stricting further Jewish immigration. At the same time, it
was added that this provision should "not be interpreted as
giving grounds for delay or postponement of the negotiation

and conclusion of the agreements for placing mandated and other territories" under the trusteeship system.

According to the Charter it will be the duty of the state administering any trust territory to insure that the territory shall play its part in the maintenance of international peace and security. To this end every such state will be empowered to make use of volunteer forces, facilities, and assistance from the trust territory "in carrying out the obligations toward the Security Council undertaken in this regard by the administering authority." This provision makes a distinct departure from the League mandates system, which expressly prohibited fortification and arming of mandated territories, but is in harmony with the concept of security embodied in the Charter, which imposes on all member states the responsibility to be prepared for fulfillment of their security obligations.

The trusteeship arrangement may designate a strategic area or areas which may include part or all of the territory to which the arrangement applies. This provision accepts the possibility, envisaged in the United States proposals, of distinguishing between strategic and non-strategic areas. In accordance with this provision, separate arrangements are made for administration of the two types of areas.

The Trusteeship Council

All functions of the organization relating to strategic areas are to be exercised by the Security Council, while all functions with regard to areas not designated as strategic are to be exercised by the General Assembly through a Trusteeship Council. The Security Council is "to avail itself" of the assistance of the Trusteeship Council to act on political, social, and economic matters in strategic areas. The Trusteeship Council is to be composed of specially qualified representatives designated in three categories: 1. One each by the states administering trust territories; 2. One each by states among the Big Five which are not administering trust territories (this provision was adopted to meet Russia's demand for its inclusion in the Trusteeship Council); 3. One each by a sufficient number of other states named for three-year periods by the General Assembly so that the total number of representatives is equally divided between administering and non-administering states. It is feared by some observers that this equal division of membership within the Trusteeship Council may result in deadlocks on crucial issues.

The General Assembly, acting through the Trusteeship Council, is empowered to consider reports submitted by the administering state, to accept petitions and examine them in consultation with the administering state, and to make periodic visits to the respective territories at times agreed upon with the administering state. The latter provision is an innovation, as the League Mandates Commission did not have the right to inspect conditions in mandated territories, and had to rely on reports from the mandatory powers. In some instances these reports were woefully inadequate, as in the case of Japan's reports about conditions in the Pacific islands over which it had mandates and which it secretly fortified before World War II. The administering authority in each trust territory is to make an annual report to the Assembly on the basis of a questionnaire formulated by the Trusteeship Council covering the political, economic, social, and educational advancement of the inhabitants of the trust territory.

In any critical consideration of the trusteeship system, it must be borne in mind that this system, although purely voluntary in character (as contrasted with the League mandates), is more flexible than the League mandates system, and could gradually be applied to all colonial territories if the Western powers want to use it for this purpose. Chapter XI, on non-self-governing peoples, is really the kernel of the section of the Charter dealing with international trusteeship, and this chapter lays down broad principles that should govern the conduct of colonial powers in dealing with dependent peoples. Moreover, the Assembly, the Security Council, the Secretary-General, and the Trusteeship Council can all bring up for consideration by the United Nations organization any colonial situation which, in their opinion, constitutes a threat to peace. Thus the Charter gives many opportunities for re-examining colonial problems in the future. At the same time, in the chapters on the international trusteeship system, it recognizes the fact that many territories which are now non-self-governing do not have, and may never develop, any realistic basis for independence.

Collective Plus Regional Security

The San Francisco conference also attempted to clarify the relationship between regional and collective security which had been left relatively obscure in the Dumbarton Oaks proposals, and had been further confused by the existence of bilateral security agreements, like the Franco-Russian alliance, and regional security pacts, notably the Act of Chapultepec concluded at the Mexico City conference. Russia, along with France, Czechoslovakia and Belgium, contended that bilateral security pacts were essential as a safeguard against the renewal of German aggression, especially during a period when the United Nations organization had not yet become firmly established as a guardian of world security. The Latin American countries, for their part, feared that on the ground of protecting their security non-American powers might seek to intervene in inter-American affairs, and argued that this would jeopardize the Monroe Doctrine and undermine Western Hemisphere solidarity.

Two compromise formulas were finally worked out to meet the special situations now existing in Europe and in the Western Hemisphere. The first formula provides that security agreements directed against former enemy states (this would include the pacts signed by Russia with Britain, France, Czechoslovakia, Poland and Yugoslavia) can be used "against renewal of aggressive policy on the part of any such state" during a transitional period, "until such time as the [United Nations] organization may, on the request of the Governments concerned, be charged with the responsibility for preventing further aggression by such a state." Europe's bilateral security pacts may thus be regarded as temporary ramparts thrown up for the period of transition during which the United Nations organization establishes a more permanent world-embracing system of security.

The second formula states that nothing in the terms of the Charter "impairs the inherent right of individual or collective self-defense if an armed attack occurs against a member of the United Nations, until the Security Council has taken the measures necessary to maintain international peace and security." Thus the Latin American countries could take measures of self-defense against one of their number resorting to aggression—but only if the Security Council has not taken action or if its action has proved inadequate. These two formulas, necessarily complex because of the complex and highly inflammable situations they sought to cover, may cause controversies when they come to be interpreted in the future.

The important thing, however, is that the primacy of collective, over bilateral and regional, security arrangements has been recognized in principle. Article 51 of the Charter provides that measures taken by member nations in the exercise of the right of self-defense shall be immediately reported to the Security Council, "and shall not in any way affect the authority and responsibility of the Security Council under the present Charter to take at any time such action as it may deem necessary in order to maintain or restore international peace and security." And Article 53 declares that security arrangements against former enemy states are an exception to the general principle that "no enforcement action shall be taken under regional arrangements or by regional agencies without the authorization of the Security Council."

Two provisions not in the Dumbarton Oaks proposals were inserted into the Charter to integrate regional and collective security arrangements. First, in Chapter VI, on the Pacific Settlement of Disputes (Article 33), the parties to any dispute endangering the maintenance of international peace and security undertake to seek a solution, among other methods, by resort to regional agencies or arrangements. Second, Chapter VII (Article 47) provides that the "Military Staff Committee, with the authorization of the Security Council and after consultation with appropriate regional agencies, may establish regional subcommittees." (This clause was especially supported by Peru.)

The International Court of Justice

The Dumbarton Oaks proposals, it will be recalled, provided for an international court of justice "which should constitute the principal judicial organ of the organization," and specified that the statute of the court should be either the statute of the Permanent Court of International Justice of 1919, "continued in force with such modifications as may be desirable," or a new statute in the preparation of which the old statute should be used as a basis. A special committee of jurists, convened in Washington on the eve of the San Francisco conference, drafted a document which may be described as the statute of the Permanent Court with certain modifications. This statute was signed by the 50 United Nations at San Francisco and, as provided at Dumbarton Oaks, is annexed to the Charter of the United Nations organization. The reconstitution of the court made it possible to exclude states which had been members of the old court, but were not members of the United Nations, notably Spain.

The three main modifications in the new statute as compared with that of 1919, are alteration of the name of the Court; inclusion of the Court in the framework of the United Nations organization; and provision for the election of its fifteen members, who are to be elected for nine-year terms by the General Assembly and by the Security Council (formerly the members were elected by the League Assembly and League Council) from a list of persons nominated by the national groups in the Permanent Court of Arbitration. Otherwise the new Court, like the old, will be located at The Hague. Its jurisdiction will again comprise only cases which the parties refer to it, except for those states which, under the "optional clause" of Article 36 of the statute declare that they recognize as compulsory the jurisdiction of the Court in four categories of legal disputes—although a number of countries urged acceptance of compulsory jurisdiction by all members. And it may give advisory opinions on any legal question at the request of whatever body may be authorized by or in accordance with the Charter of the United Nations to make such a request. Article 36 of the Charter states that, in making recommendations about the pacific settlement of disputes, the Security Council should take into consideration "that legal disputes should as a general rule be referred by the parties to the International Court of Justice in accordance with the provisions of the Statute of the Court." Since the Court is open only to states, not to individuals, it is doubtful that it will be able to investigate violations of the human rights proclaimed in the Charter.

Provisions for Amendment

As President Truman said in his address at the closing session of the UNCIO on June 26, the Charter "has not been poured into a fixed mold." Changing world conditions "will require readjustments—but they will be the readjustments of peace and not of war." The Charter provides that if a general conference to review the document has not been held before the tenth annual session of the General Assembly, a proposal to that effect shall be placed on the agenda of that session. A general conference to review the Charter can be summoned at any time by a two-thirds vote of the General Assembly (in the tenth year and after by a majority vote) and by a vote of any seven members of the Security Council. The provision regarding the Security Council vote on this subject—"any seven members" —was adopted so as to prevent the possibility, feared by the middle and small nations that, if unanimity of the permanent members was required, any one of the Big Five might veto the calling of a reviewing conference. Since there are six non-permanent members of the Council, the vote of only one permanent member will be required. Any alteration of the Charter recommended by a two-thirds vote of the conference shall take effect when ratified by two-thirds of the members of the United Nations including all the permanent members of the Security Council. It is conceivable that at this stage one of the Big Five may veto ratification of an amendment—but in practice such a development is less likely than a Big Five veto over the initiation of amendments.

An official interpretative report, which is not a part of the Charter but is included in the record of the conference, links amendments to the conditions under which member states may withdraw from the organization—a matter not covered by the Dumbarton Oaks proposals. It is understood that member states may withdraw under at least three conditions: if, in their opinion, the organization has not maintained peace with justice; if it has adopted amendments unacceptable to the withdrawing state; and, most important of all, if amendments adopted by a general conference of the United Nations fail to come into effect because of the veto of any one of the Big Five. The third of these conditions gives the middle and small nations a sort of counter-veto against any one of the Big Five which seeks to prevent the ratification of amendments. It is even conceivable that a majority of the United Nations, including possibly three or four of the Big Five, could withdraw en masse from the organization and form a new one based on the same principles. A precedent in this respect was set by members of the Permanent Court of International Justice who reorganized themselves into the practically identical International Court of Justice, leaving out nations regarded as unwelcome in the new group, notably Franco Spain.

The Charter is to be ratified by the 50 signatory states in accordance with their respective constitutional processes, and is to come into force upon the deposit of ratifications with the government of the United States by the Big Five and by a majority of the other signatories. On July 2 President Truman submitted the Charter to the Senate, with an urgent plea that the United States should be the first to ratify this document, thus assuring the world that this time we are determined to cooperate with other nations in peace, just as effectively as we have in war. Mr. Stettinius, who on June 27 resigned as Secretary of State to become American delegate to the United Nations organization, served as the President's representative before the Senate Foreign Relations Committee as it considered the Charter.

Interim Commission

Pending the coming into force of the Charter and the establishment of the United Nations organization, which is to be known as the United Nations, the 50 signatory states, in an agreement signed at San Francisco on June 26, created an interim Preparatory Commission. This Commission, which is to be located in London, will be composed of one representative from each of the 50 signatory states. It will function through an executive committee composed of representatives of those states who were represented on the executive committee of the San Francisco conference.

The Preparatory Commission, which opened its sessions in London in August 1945, is to make provisional arrangements for the first sessions of the General Assembly, the Security Council, the Economic and Social Council and the Trusteeship Council, for the establishment of the Secretariat, and for the convening of the International Court of

Justice. It will also formulate recommendations for the possible transfer of certain functions, activities and assets of the League of Nations which it may be desirable for the new organization to take over; and examine the problems involved in the establishment of the relationship between specialized intergovernmental organizations and agencies and the United Nations organization. The latter provision will present a number of problems, especially in establishing the relationship of the organization with the International Labor Office, an autonomous tripartite organization established in 1919 in which governments, employers, and workers are represented, and of which Russia, although invited to join in 1943, is not a member. The Preparatory Commission will cease to exist upon the election of the Secretary-General of the United Nations organization, at which time its property and records will be transferred to the organization. These interim arrangements make it certain that during the period of six months or longer that may be required for ratification by the number of states necessary to make the Charter operative, the task of organizing the work of the organization will be carried forward without interruption.

Attitude of United States

In contrast to 1919, when minority opposition to American participation in the League of Nations was far more vocal than the widespread popular support for the League Covenant, public opinion during World War II increasingly favored this country's cooperation with the other United Nations in the post-war period; and these views were reflected in the utterances of many Senators. The Dumbarton Oaks proposals, moreover, had been laid before the people of the United States (as well as of the other United Nations) six months in advance of the San Francisco conference, in contrast to the situation in 1919, when the League Covenant was presented as a finished document for ratification by the Senate after the Paris Peace conference, in spite of Congressional warning that the League of Nations should not be linked to the peace settlements. The San Francisco Charter not only defined the area of agreement among 50 nations, but was also a clear expression of American policy already formally stated in the Fulbright (House) and Connally (Senate) resolutions.

Moreover, the participation of Senators Vandenberg (Republican) and Connally (Democrat) in the San Francisco negotiations assured that the Senate would approach the Charter in a non-partisan spirit. The Senate's discussion was facilitated by the fact that the Charter contains a statement of general principles concerning justice, human welfare, and observance of international law; gives the Big Five a veto over enforcement action; makes a declaration regarding the treatment of dependent peoples; and assures possibilities of amendment in due course. These provisions, some of which were absent from the Dumbarton Oaks proposals, went far to meet any possible objections to the Charter such as were raised by a number of Senators about the League Covenant in 1919. It was a foregone conclusion, under the circumstances, that the Charter would secure the two-thirds vote in the Senate necessary for ratification. And it was ratified by the Senate on July 28 by a vote of 89 to 2.

This overwhelming ratification does not mean, however, that the road to effective cooperation with other nations is now clear. Ratification of the Charter is only the first and easiest step because it requires no concrete action by the United States which might be interpreted by critics as a

"sacrifice" of national interests. Difficulties may be anticipated when discussion turns to implementation of the
Charter. Four points, particularly, may arouse debate in
Congress: specification of the armed forces the United
States will place at the disposal of the organization by a
special agreement or agreements to be negotiated with the
Security Council; the scope of the authority to be exercised
by the American delegate to the Security Council, who may
be called upon to vote for the use of American forces against
an aggressor; the provisions in the chapter on non-self-
governing peoples which calls for periodic reports to the
United Nations organization by member states—provisions
that may bring objections if applied to Puerto Rico, Hawaii,
and Alaska, and especially to islands in the Pacific that may
be placed under trusteeship; and the proposal made by some
that the United States accept the compulsory jurisdiction of
the International Court of Justice.

A Tool, Not a Panacea

Criticism may come not only from those who may think
the United Nations organization requires too much from its
members, and will therefore prove too domineering, but
also from those who believe that it requires too little, and
will therefore prove impotent. It is true that the United
Nations organization is far from being a world state. Nor
will we have a world state until nations are ready to abandon
the concept of sovereignty. The Security Council, therefore,
although far stronger on paper than the League Council,
will still depend in practice on sovereign member nations,
as Mr. Stettinius stated in his report to President Truman, "for
the weapons both of persuasion and of force through which
it will attempt to keep the peace." For the same reason the

General Assembly is a forum for debate, not a legislature that can legislate for member nations; the Economic and Social Council can recommend measures to member nations, but cannot enforce their application; and the International Court of Justice has only limited jurisdiction. The United Nations organization is not a universal panacea. It is a tool whose efficacy will depend entirely on the willingness of nations to use it in the tasks of maintaining peace and alleviating the causes of war.

Just as the United States led the way in transforming the wartime coalition of the United Nations into a peacetime organization beginning with the Moscow conference and ending with that of San Francisco, so it will be in a strategic position to lead in the far more difficult task of implementing the Charter. A document cannot of itself prevent war or check aggression. If not used, it will become atrophied. Only through the give-and-take of daily negotiations, compromises and adjustments in the various agencies of the United Nations organization shall we be able to weave the web of mutual interests which is essential to the existence of any human society, and is ultimately a greater safeguard against war than the most ingenious and costly armaments.

CHAPTER V

POTSDAM AND AFTER

THE Potsdam Declaration, issued on August 2 at the close of what history is to know as the Berlin conference, had as its central theme the liquidation of Germany's military power and its industrial potentialities to wage war in the future. Germany was not broken up into three or four states, as had been proposed earlier by some Allied commentators. The Big Three agreed that in the four zones of occupation (American, British, Russian and French) uniform treatment shall be accorded to the German population "so far as is practicable"; and that during the period of occupation Germany shall be treated as a single economic unit. The unification of the Allies' policy toward Germany, which was urgently needed, is thus provided for.

But German territory does not remain intact. It is in reality split into two areas—the area east of the Oder, which is to be divided between Russia and Poland, "pending final determination" of their respective western frontiers; and the area west of the Oder, divided into the four Allied zones of occupation. Most of East Prussia, cradle of Prussian militarism, including the city of Koenigsberg, is assigned to Russia. The remainder of East Prussia, the port of Danzig (a bone of contention between Germany and Poland during the inter-war years), and Silesia, rich in coal and industrial installations, is assigned to Poland—in compensation for Eastern Poland, taken by Russia in 1939. This territorial exchange had been approved, in principle, at the Yalta conference. In spite of France's often proclaimed desire for the Rhineland, no territorial cessions in the west were envisaged in the Potsdam Declaration.

Territorial Cessions Create Future Threat

No one familiar with the sufferings and depredations inflicted by the Germans on neighboring nations would urge a "soft peace," or any arrangement calculated to perpetuate Germany's military power. But it may well be asked whether the Big Three have not made to Poland a dubious and potentially dangerous gift. True, the Potsdam Declaration provides for the transfer of German populations not only from Poland but also from Hungary and Czechoslovakia (which remembers all too vividly the problem created by the presence of three and a half million Sudeten Germans within its borders). This transfer, which will at least forestall agitation by German minority groups for reunion with the Reich, was already under way. The Big Three, however, agreed that any transfers that take place "should be effected in an orderly and humane manner"; and requested the governments of Germany's three eastern neighbors to suspend further expulsions until they have had time to examine the reports of their representatives on the Allied Control Council concerning the time and rate at which "further transfers could be carried out having regard to the present situation in Germany."

Germany's territorial losses and the transfer to the Reich of German populations estimated at between 10 and 15 million are bound to have serious repercussions on the German economy, whose activities are drastically curtailed by the Potsdam Declaration. It was to be expected that all production of items "directly necessary to a war economy" would be "rigidly controlled and restricted to Germany's approved post-war peacetime needs": that productive capacity not needed for permitted production would be removed or destroyed; and that the production of arms, ammunition, and implements of war would be prohibited and prevented. In view of the monopolistic, far-reaching control exercised by certain German industries through cartels and other arrangements, it was also to be expected that provision would be made for decentralization of German economy.

Two Zones of Reparations

For the collection of reparations Germany is again divided into two areas. Russia is free to remove food, machinery, tools, and so on from the area it occupies, with the proviso that out of its share it is to settle Poland's claims to reparations. The claims of the United States, Britain, and other countries "entitled to reparations" (including, presumably, France) are to be met from the zones occupied by the Western powers and from Germany's assets abroad. Russia, already rich in gold, makes no claim to gold captured by the Allies in Germany; but it is accorded 25 percent of reparations from the western zone. Of this share 15 percent, to be collected "in the first place" from the metallurgical, chemical, and machine-manufacturing industries "unnecessary for the German peace economy," is to be exchanged for an equivalent value of food, coal, potash, timber, petroleum, and so on from the Russian-occupied zone; and 10 percent is to be transferred to Russia on account of reparations without payment or exchange of any kind.

The Potsdam Declaration provides that, in organizing the German economy, "primary emphasis shall be given to the development of agriculture and peaceful domestic industries." This is a desirable objective, provided Germany retains areas capable of producing sufficient food for its population. It is in this connection, particularly, that the assignment of Germany's richest agricultural areas in the east to Poland and Russia, plus the transfer of several million Germans into an agriculturally impoverished Reich, raise serious questions as to the viability of the economic plans drawn up for post-war Germany.

The aim of Berlin conferees—an aim that will have the hearty approval of all of Germany's victims—is "to maintain in Germany living standards not exceeding the average of the standards of living of European countries" (exclusive of Britain and Russia). This is important if Germany's neighbors are to recover from the losses of manpower, technical skill, and productive resources they suffered during the war. But the European countries which proved economically and militarily unable to resist Germany will benefit only negatively from arrangements projected for Germany's economy unless the Big Three help them to develop their economies to the level attainable by the technically superior Germans; and provide them also with the manufactured goods they need, in quantities and at prices comparable to the terms that might otherwise be offered by a peaceable German industry. The Potsdam Declaration provides in every conceivable way for methods to make Germany weak. But it is strikingly barren of provisions to make the rest of Europe strong.

Such provisions must find a place in future agreements to be negotiated by the Council of Ministers of the Big Five, created at the Berlin conference, which is to have its head-quarters in London. This Council had as its first task the drawing up of peace treaties with other ex-enemy countries—Italy, Rumania, Hungary, and Bulgaria. But in the course of settling Allied accounts with Germany and its satellites, we must not forget the needs and aspirations of countries in Europe which bore the brunt of German aggression and are now struggling with painful problems of rehabilitation. It would be comforting to believe that Germany's lightning conquest of Europe was due solely to its superior military and industrial power. But the trial of Marshal Pétain, the memoirs of Reynaud, the diaries of Ciano, all underline a lesson we should have learned long ago: that fundamental political and economic weaknesses in countries attacked or threatened by the Germans greatly facilitated Hitler's initial victories. These weaknesses must be clearly understood and unremittingly corrected if we are to give the Germans an example of how to reconstruct their life on "a democratic and peaceful basis," as provided in the Potsdam Declaration; and if we are to discover for ourselves how to assure conditions of security and stability for the rest of the world.

Problems Ahead in Europe

On the periphery of Germany, too, the Allies face serious tests of their determination to collaborate in time of peace as they had in time of war. Will Britain, which depends on international trade and finance for the maintenance of its position as a world power and the kernel of a great empire, succeed in re-establishing its economic position, gravely undermined by the material sacrifices it had been forced to make during the war? Will its efforts to effect economic recovery meet with opposition on the part of the United States, whose vastly increased industries offer a formidable competition to Britain in world markets? Or will this country find it to its advantage to strengthen Britain economically, so that Britain can remain not only a loyal, but a friendly, ally in the post-war period? Will Britain's strategic interests in the Mediterranean, from Spain, where it has hesitated to apply outright pressure against the Franco regime, to Greece, where under Churchill it favored restoration of a conservative monarchy, clash with those of Russia, which is seeking control of outlets to the high seas, notably the Dardanelles, and has favored the formation in the Balkans and Eastern Europe of governments "friendly" to Moscow? Will Britain claim Italy's colonies in Africa as its share of the spoils of war, as the United States claims Japanese islands in the Pacific, and Russia claims adjoining territories in Europe and Asia? Or will the Italian colonies be turned over to the United Nations organization as a trust for civilization? Will international waterways like the Suez and Panama Canals, and the Dardanelles, be placed under international control? Many of these questions were either touched upon at Potsdam, or were in the back of the minds of the delegates as they mapped out their terms for Germany, but were left to subsequent conferences for discussion.

Ultimatum to Japan

From Potsdam, too, the United States, Britain and China, advised by Russia of Japan's request for mediation by Moscow, issued an ultimatum to Japan. This ultimatum demanded total disarmament, the punishment of war criminals, the break-up of the Japanese empire, and the end of war industry. In contrast to the terms imposed on Germany, however, it promised a limited occupation (confined to designated points), territorial integrity of the home islands, access to raw materials from abroad, eventual participation in world trade, and withdrawal of the occupying forces after the accomplishment of Allied objectives and after "there has been established in accordance with the freely expressed will of the Japanese people a peacefully inclined and responsible government." When Japan, although warned that new weapons of warfare would be used against it, rejected the Potsdam ultimatum, the atomic bomb was used for the first time in history on August 5 against the Japanese city of Hiroshima; and on August 6 President Truman told the Japanese that, if they did not accept the Potsdam terms, they could "expect a rain of ruin from the air, the like of which has never been seen on this earth." Two days later, on August 8, Russia declared war on Japan and subscribed to the terms presented to Tokyo by its three great allies. On August 10 Japan, in a note to the Big Four, accepted the Potsdam ultimatum "with the understanding that the said declaration does not comprise any demand which prejudices the prerogatives of His Majesty as a sovereign ruler." The reply of the Big Four, issued on their behalf by the United States on August 11, stated that the Emperor's authority was to "be subject to the Supreme Commander of the Allied Powers, who will take such steps as he deems proper to effectuate the surrender terms." The Emperor, whom the Japanese have worshipped as a god, is to serve as an instrument of the Supreme Commander, General MacArthur, while "the ultimate form of government of Japan" is to rest on "the freely expressed will of the Japanese people." These terms Japan accepted on August 14, and the surrender was signed on the U.S.S. *Missouri* on September 1, the anniversary of Germany's invasion of Poland.

Russo-Chinese Settlement

As in the case of Germany, Japan's surrender leaves many problems for the Allies to settle in the post-war period. Not only will they have to devise ways and means of giving scope for the free expression of the "will of the Japanese people," and assure Japan sufficient livelihood to prevent that country from again seeking relief from its economic problems in wars of aggression, but they will have to cope with the multifarious issues raised by the return to the Western powers and to China of territories seized by Japan. A long step toward settlement of outstanding issues between Russia and China which, it had been feared, might disturb Asia for years to come, was taken with the conclusion in Moscow on August 26 of a thirty-year pact of friendship and alliance between the two countries. The most significant features of the treaty and its six supplementary agreements are the recognition of a special position for Russia in Manchuria and the explicit pledge of the signatories "to act according to the principles of mutual respect for their sovereignty and territorial entity and non-interference in the internal affairs of both contracting parties." The U.S.S.R. thus made it clear that it intends to deal only with the Chinese Central government and will not extend aid or recognition to the Chinese Communists at Yenan. Shortly after conversations looking toward national unity were opened in Chungking by Generalissimo Chiang Kai-shek and Mao Tse-tung, leader of the Chinese Communists.

The Russo-Chinese agreements did not restore Russia to the position it occupied before the Russo-Japanese war of

1904-05. The rights granted to the U.S.S.R. by China are much more limited than those possessed by Tsarist Russia, and do not include extraterritoriality. Russia and China are to have joint control of the Chinese Eastern Railway and the South Manchuria Railway, which are to be combined under the single name of the Chinese Changchun Railway. The joint control, however, applies only to those properties in which the Russians previously had an interest, and other lines will apparently come under complete Chinese control. Port Arthur is to be used jointly by both countries as a naval base "at the disposal of the battleships and merchant ships of China and the U.S.S.R. alone," while the near-by port of Dairen is to be "a free port open to trade and shipping of all countries." In Dairen various piers and warehouses will be leased to Russia, and no import or export duties will be levied on goods passing directly to or from the Soviet Union through the port. In both Port Arthur and Dairen the civil administration is to be Chinese, but there will be a large measure of Russian authority, especially in the former.

The Soviet government has declared that it regards Manchuria as part of China, and undertakes to respect China's full sovereignty over that area. According to a minute appended to the treaty, Premier Stalin pledged that Russian troops would begin to withdraw from Manchuria three weeks after Japan's capitulation, the withdrawal to be completed within three months at the most. With regard to Outer Mongolia, which is non-Chinese in language, population and historical background, but in theory has been under Chinese sovereignty, it is agreed that if a plebiscite confirms the people's desire for independence, China will recognize Outer Mongolia's independent status. It is expected that

Outer Mongolia will vote for independence, and in an address of August 25 Generalissimo Chiang Kai-shek declared that recognition of its independence was not only necessary for friendship, but would also be in harmony with the Kuomintang's principles of the equality and freedom of peoples. In connection with Sinkiang, a border area in the far northwest in which the Russians exerted great influence from 1934 to 1942, Russian Foreign Commissar Molotov stated that the Soviet Union "has no intention to interfere with China's internal affairs." This declaration referred specifically to "the latest events in Sinkiang," i.e., presumably to reported clashes between Central forces and local insurgents.

Problems Ahead in Asia

While a settlement has thus been reached between Russia and China, and the United States has tacitly agreed to Russia's occupation of the Kurile Islands and of southern Sakhalin, many other questions are in process of discussion. Will Britain retain Hong Kong, on whose development it has spent much money and effort? What measures will China take to protect the rights and interests of foreigners now that extraterritoriality has ended, notably in centers of foreign commerce like Shanghai? Will Thailand be treated as a friend of the United Nations, as the United States regards it, or as a collaborator of Japan, the view taken by Britain? Will France's title to Indo-China be restored without a struggle, or will native nationalists challenge French colonial rule? What kind of arrangement will Britain's Labor government offer to India? Will any one of the United Nations avail itself of the possibility, envisaged in the San Francisco Charter, of placing its colonies under the trusteeship of the United Nations organization? And how will the United States dispose of the islands it has occupied in the Pacific—both those formerly owned by Germany which had been mandated to Japan by the League of Nations in 1919, and those owned outright by Japan, like Okinawa? No sooner had the "cease fire" order been heard in the Pacific, than the Allies had begun to be confronted with these and other issues.

Pessimists doubt that the United Nations will be able to resolve the problems that face them in Europe and Asia without arousing mutual resentments and suspicions that might lead to future wars. And obviously unless the will to settle these problems by peaceful means exists on the part of all concerned, the machinery of international collaboration set up at San Francisco will prove futile.

How Will Atomic Bomb and War as a Crime Affect U. S. Policy?

At the same time the use of the atomic bomb has shocked mankind into realizing that this newest weapon of war, unless rigidly controlled by the nations who possess its secret, can be used not only to shorten war—as was done in Japan— but can spell destruction for large areas of the world. Terrible as are the potentialities of the atomic bomb, we must not waste time in deprecating its use. Instead, we must be more determined than ever to prevent the recurrence of war. For once we admit, as some people do, that war is natural or inevitable, then it becomes difficult to denounce any weapons, no matter how destructive or horrifying, which may be used to prosecute it, and even to shorten the agony of modern warfare. Aggressive war itself is a crime; the particular weapons used to wage it at any given time in history are merely accessories after the fact.

War Must Be Recognized as a Crime

This is why the announcement on August 8 in London that representatives of the United States, Britain, Russia, and France had accepted Justice Robert H. Jackson's formula that war is a crime, for which its instigators and perpetrators can be tried as war criminals, is potentially as revolutionary and far-reaching in its implications as the discovery of the atomic bomb. Although thus far restricted to the European Axis countries, this concept could, if consistently applied by the United Nations to any future aggressors, provide the safeguard we need against the abuse of mankind's scientific genius for destructive ends.

So far there has been real danger of our seemingly limitless capacity for invention and machine production hopelessly outrunning our capacity to control relations between nations. Social scientists have seemed timorous, barren of new ideas, and unduly addicted to cenventional patterns as compared with their colleagues working in the laboratories of universities and factories. In a series of agreements nations have feebly tried to humanize and regulate war—as if anything so essentially inhuman as war could be made tolerable in the machine age. True, the signatories of the Kellogg-Briand Pact of 1928 agreed to outlaw war as an instrument of national policy—but with so many reservations, explicit and implicit, as to invalidate that pact from the outset. Yet here was the seed the United Nations War Crimes Commission is trying to bring to fruition. For as Justice Jackson has cogently argued, if war is outlawed, then those who provoke war are outside the pale of law, and should be treated as criminals. If war is recognized by mankind as a crime, and shorn of honor as it has already been shorn of glory, history may record our so far brutal century as a new era in human relations.

World Organization Needed More than Ever

How will these two simultaneous discoveries—the atomic bomb and the concept of war as a crime—affect the foreign policy of the United States? The new bomb gives added evidence, if this were needed, that isolation is impossible. The long-range bomber, the use of V-1 and V-2 bombs and jet planes, had already demonstrated the ineffectiveness of frontiers and static fortifications against attacks on a nation's territory. Now the United States, Britain, and Canada possess the secret of a weapon which could play havoc with land and sea defenses, as well as with the industrial resources necessary to wage modern war. It is fortunate, from our point of view, that the secret is held by three democratic countries which, in modern times, have shown no predilection for militarism; and President Truman, in his broadcast of August 9, indicated that the three countries intended to keep their secret until adequate controls against its misuse had been devised.

But the United States cannot prevent other countries from pursuing similar scientific research and arriving sooner or later at similar results. In fact, the use of weapons like the atomic bomb may cause interesting shifts in the balance of power worked out by the Big Three. For, as Brig. Gen. David Sarnoff, president of the Radio Corporation of America, has pointed out, small nations skilled in scientific research would have as deadly a power at their command as the great nations, provided they were ready to make the necessary expenditures; and money invested in laboratories might seem to them a more productive investment than money spent on inevitably ineffective land, naval, or air forces. It is therefore more than ever in the interest of the United States—and the other great powers—to speed the establishment of a strong and responsible international organization in which smaller nations would feel assured of protection against attack. In fact, instead of jealously withholding a scientific secret which will eventually be penetrated by other countries, the United States would be well advised to place it at the disposal of the United Nations organization, requesting, as an essential *quid pro quo*, that the organization should be granted stronger controls over its members than it possesses under the San Francisco Charter.

Our Ideals Must Shape Policy

The discovery of the atomic bomb also enhances the need for the United States to harmonize its practices in foreign affairs more closely than in the past with its professed ideals. This country has the power to make itself feared. It can exercise its power constructively only if it succeeds in making itself trusted. The weakness of American foreign policy has been that, frequently, when faced with concrete situations, we have seemed to fall short of our ideals, which have served as inspiration to other peoples. What are the roots of these ideals? The Swedish sociologist, Gunnar Myrdal, looking dispassionately at the "American Creed," has pointed out that this country, born of revolution, has felt an instinctive sympathy for revolutionary movements elsewhere, especially in the colonies; that even the values we are conservative about—that we seek to conserve—are liberal values; and that Americans, more than any other people, think in moral terms and are concerned about social justice, even though we do not always achieve it at home. Our primary endeavor in the atomic age, the age when war may become punishable as a crime, is to translate these features of the American Creed into foreign policy.

Our task during the war years has been rendered difficult by the fact that the government of one of our principal allies, Britain, seemed averse to fundamental change both in Europe and Asia; and that, in trying to cooperate with Britain, we made it possible for Russia to become a mouth-piece for the changes we would otherwise have favored, or at least have accepted. This potential conflict between Britain and Russia made the position of the United States both ambiguous and lacking in inspiration for the peoples of Europe and Asia who hoped to find here leadership in the advancement of political and economic democracy. The victory of the British Labor party has removed one obstacle to the application of our ideals in foreign policy; and if the United States and Britain now jointly support individuals and groups throughout the world who try to root out fascism, Russia will no longer be able to act as sole pro-ponent of anti-fascism. This equalization in the roles of the three great powers should greatly facilitate orderly demo-cratic reform both in Europe and Asia.

Scientists have shown us that nothing is impossible for those who have the will to succeed. There is no reason to assume that human relations are more subject to limitations than scientific discovery.

Can We Escape the Vicious Circle?

Once more, as the iron controls of the war years are relaxed, we face the vicious circle mentioned by British Foreign Secretary Bevin in his address to the House of Commons on August 20: lack of trade endangers security, and lack of security endangers trade. Economic reconstruction of the liberated areas is an essential prerequisite to their political reconstruction, and especially to the development of institutions that the United States and Britain would regard as democratic. Yet economics cannot be divorced from or put ahead of politics. We have seen this clearly in the case of the British elections when, the moment Labor's sweeping victory became known, some Americans immediately questioned the advisability of economic aid to a country where political changes might result in limitations on free enterprise. The termination of lend-lease aid to Britain, announced by the United States on August 21, was in accordance with the terms of the law, which provided for termination of such aid at the end of the war. But the feeling of near-despair that this action then produced in Britain shows—if evidence were needed—that ratification of documents like the United Nations Charter and the Bretton Woods agreements are not enough to assure world security and stability. We now have to put concrete content into these documents through consultation with other United Nations concerning our mutual needs.

The United States, as Mr. Churchill said on August 16, "stands at the summit of the world." Our decisions, as well as our indecisions, will profoundly affect economic and political developments all over the globe. It is natural that we should think first of all about ourselves—about the resumption of our own production and improvement of our living standards. But it would be unfortunate if absorption in affairs at home should cause us to forget that timely, well-considered aid now to countries teetering on the verge of economic breakdown and political anarchy would go far to avert the danger of another costly conflict.

The very fact that we possess the economic power to foster or delay the reconstruction of devastated and impoverished areas raises the question of how we might use this power to promote and strengthen political democracy. Mr. Bevin appeared to agree with Mr. Churchill that conditions now existing in Eastern Europe and the Balkans are not favorable to democracy. In fact, commenting on the situation in Hungary, Rumania, and Bulgaria, he said that "one kind of totalitarianism is being replaced by another." Both the United States and Britain criticized arrangements for the Bulgarian elections—originally scheduled to be held on August 26 but then postponed "to a later date"—on the ground that they did not insure free expression of the wishes of the people; and both have indicated that they intend to see to it that the references to democracy contained in United Nations documents from the Atlantic Charter to the Potsdam Declaration do not remain a dead letter.

How Can We Advance Democracy?

How can the Western powers most effectively carry out their pledges to liberated peoples in Europe and Asia? Today there is no more pretense in Washington and London, as there was in the days of the Spanish Civil War, that the Western democracies are pursuing a policy of "nonintervention" and, like Pilate, can wash their hands of the internal affairs of other nations. Today the United States and Britain are committed to intervention on behalf of democracy, against totalitarianism of both Right and Left. When American and British spokesmen criticize Russia's activities in Eastern Europe and the Balkans, then it must be assumed that they oppose not Russia's intervention *per se,* since the United States and Britain also claim the right to intervene, but the fact that Russia is said to support individuals or groups whom the Western powers regard as inimical to democracy.

The "very much overworked word democracy," as Mr. Bevin has said, "appears to need definition." There is little doubt that the Russians, in all the countries they helped to liberate from the Nazis, have directly or indirectly favored the workers and peasants, who in these countries form a majority of the population, against former government administrators, landowners, and owners of factories, mines, and other large-scale property. This, certainly, is not political democracy as we know it in the United States and Britain. But neither is it political democracy in our sense of the term when, as has frequently happened in the past, the United States and Britain tend to deal with owners of land and factories, who in Eastern Europe and the Balkans represent a minority of the population, and show little or no concern for the welfare and interests of the rest of the population. We deplore, and quite rightly, the excesses that have accompanied liberation of many nations in Europe. But we forget that both we and the British passed through revolutions and civil wars before we succeeded in establishing stable democratic institutions.

The questions we, along with the British, are asking about elections in Eastern Europe and the Balkans sound more convincing since the United States has begun to question dictatorships of the Right, as well as the Left. Nelson Rockefeller, in his swan-song speech before the Pan-American Society in Boston on August 24, flayed the abuses of the Farrell government. Yet these abuses were known to the

State Department in April, when the United States recognized that government and vigorously urged Argentina's admission to the San Francisco conference in opposition to Russia's demand for postponement. It must be hoped that the appointment of Spruille Braden, former ambassador to Buenos Aires who has been critical of the Argentine government, as Assistant Secretary of State in charge of Latin American affairs, succeeding Nelson Rockefeller, will harmonize our policy of intervention on behalf of democracy in Europe with our policy in Latin America, which has seemed unduly tolerant of dictatorships. And it must be hoped that in Japan, too, General MacArthur, using the Emperor as his instrument, will foster the emergence of popular movements, and curtail the power of feudal militarists and their allies among reactionary industrialists.

There is no simple answer to any of the questions left in the wake of Potsdam. Too many emotions, fears, and prejudices are clustered about the word "democracy," as the Big Three have been using it, to permit of dogmatic definitions. But if by democracy we mean in essence a way of life that makes it possible for human beings of all races, creeds, and economic conditions to work together with as little deference to economic or political privilege as it is humanly possible to achieve—then it is not impossible for the Big Three eventually to find a common meeting ground for their respective aspirations. We must not let such embers of freedom as existed in Eastern Europe and the Balkans be extinguished in the hour of liberation. But we can fan them into a steady flame only if we ourselves are determined to play no favorites and to see to it that free elections lead to, and not away from, economic and social reforms. The experience of Russia, understandable in terms of that country's history of autocratic political rule and economic backwardness, was not a guide for most of Europe west of the Vistula. Yet in the absence of constructive leadership on the part of Britain and the United States there was serious danger that a feeling of futility and despair would spread over the continent like a creeping paralysis, and destroy the last vestiges of democracy. The Labor victory in Britain and the firmness of the United States toward the dictatorships of Argentina and Spain have heartened the moderates—and the post-war world urgently needs strong middle groups which are eager to work for social progress, but unwilling to sacrifice human liberties in the process of achieving it.

CHAPTER VI

THE AMERICAN VOTER AND INTER-NATIONAL ORGANIZATION

THE success of the United Nations organization will depend, we now see, on the willingness of the nations composing it to make it work. This will be particularly true of the United States because this country, now that the war is over, not only has at its disposal the greatest industrial and financial resources of any nation in the world, but, because it has no extensive territorial ambitions, will be in a peculiarly favorable position to maintain a balance between the conflicting interests of other great powers, to play the role of disinterested mediator.

But even those of us who sincerely want the United States to play this role, and to cooperate with other nations in all fields of endeavor, do not always understand the difficulties of developing such a policy. This country until recently had been acting in world affairs as if it had not moved much beyond the stage it occupied when the thirteen colonies joined into a Federal Union. We are more accustomed to making unilateral declarations of policy, such as the Monroe Doctrine and the policy of the "Open Door," than to taking action in concert with other nations. The very fact that the United States has traditionally avoided alliances has fostered a habit on our part of making our own decisions, and then proclaiming them to the world; yet we resent it when other great powers, for example Britain or Russia, do the same thing, and we demand to be consulted. The only important exception to this tradition of ours—and that only during the past decade—has been our policy of consultation with Latin American countries and Canada on problems of the Western Hemisphere. This Good Neighbor policy marks great progress as compared with our attitude toward the League of Nations. But it is still difficult to make Americans realize that if we are to develop a cooperative foreign policy, we shall have to learn to consult continuously with other nations; listen to their grievances, just as we tell them ours; make compromises they urge, just as we ask them to make compromises. We have to learn that our own ideals and desires, no matter how noble they seem to us, cannot be carried out in practice if this country acts alone. And if we want to enlist the cooperation of other nations in carrying them out, we shall have to take into consideration *their* ideals and desires, which may not always be the same as ours. This applies, too, to the international system of collective security. We cannot impose our conception of an ideal system on the rest of the world. We must build it in concert with other nations.

If we do not always succeed in achieving the goal for which we set out, we have no right to become disheartened and to denounce other nations. We cannot expect to win every time, and we should be able to display in international relations the good sportsmanship for which we are noted in contests of physical skill. Nor should be approach all international negotiations with the jaundiced expectation that the other fellow is smarter than we are and will always outwit us. Americans have proved over and over again that they are remarkably efficient in the ways of the modern industrial world, that they are shrewd in business transactions, and have no need to fear the competition of other nations at the conference table if they only take the trouble to inform themselves in advance about the subject under discussion. The record of history goes to show that in the contests we have had with other nations—in the fields of arbitration and trade as well as on the field of battle—the United States has seldom come out the loser.

Domestic Machinery Needed for Cooperation

But difficult as it will be for us to become accustomed to the idea of cooperating with other nations in the common enterprise of peacetime construction, we can greatly ease this task by developing at home the constitutional machinery necessary to make cooperation effective. Under our present system the Executive—that is, the President and the Department of State, whose head he appoints with the consent of the Senate—is charged with the conduct of this country's relations with other nations. These relations have expanded immeasurably since the foundation of the Republic, especially in the war years, and now call for complex negotiations on a wide range of economic and technical as well as political problems. Nor are these negotiations conducted with only one nation at a time, but with forty or fifty nations, as at the Hot Springs Food conference, the Atlantic City conference on relief and rehabilitation, the Bretton Woods conference, the Chicago Aviation conference, the conferences of Mexico City and San Francisco. But mere negotiations obviously will lead nowhere unless their results are finally embodied in concrete undertakings by the participating nations. It is when the President and the State Department present to Congress treaties or agreements providing for action by the United States that our willingness to cooperate with other nations comes to a crucial test.

Why the Senate Ratifies Treaties

As we all know, treaties entered into by the United States must be approved by the Senate before they can go into effect, and approval requires a vote by two-thirds of the Senators present and voting. In all cases in which appropriations are required the consent of the House of Representatives, where bills concerning financial matters originate, must also be obtained. The drafters of the Constitution adopted the two-thirds rule to protect the various states, which at that time had conflicting sectional interests. This reason disappeared long ago with the unification of the country and the centralization of responsibility for the conduct of foreign relations in the Federal government. Approval of treaties was entrusted to the Senate instead of Congress as a whole, first, to make it possible to act on treaties with secrecy and dispatch; and second, to make sure that the judgment of cooler heads in the Senate would prevail over possible hotheads in the House. The first reason now has little importance by the time a treaty or agreement is submitted to the Senate, since it is the preparatory negotiations that require secrecy, not the agreed document, which is usually given wide publicity a considerable time before the Senate takes any action on it. The Dumbarton Oaks document, for example, was purposely given wide publicity by the State Department so as to acquaint the American public with its terms, and by the time it had been re-drafted at San Francisco into the Charter of the United Nations there was nothing very secret about the whole transaction. The second reason seems less convincing today than two centuries ago, for now the voters are often more troubled by the procrastination of the Senate than by the possible impetuosity of the House.

The fact, however, that the Senate is seldom thoroughly informed in advance about negotiations leading to the drafting of treaties, and is instead suddenly confronted with a completed text, is one of the main reasons for the frequently hostile attitude of that body toward treaties submitted to it by the Executive, no matter which political party happens to be in power. Secretary of State John Hay under the Republican administration of Theodore Roosevelt had just as much trouble getting treaties through the Senate as Woodrow Wilson had in obtaining fair consideration of the Versailles Treaty embodying the League of Nations Covenant.

The Senate's reaction to any treaty or agreement presented for ratification is often automatically one of suspicion. It is true that the Senate has not rejected many treaties outright. But among the treaties it rejected were important documents providing for United States participation in international organization—notably the League of Nations Covenant and the Statute of the Permanent Court of International Justice. Many treaties, moreover, never reach the floor, having been pigeonholed by the powerful Senate Foreign Relations Committee. It should be noted that the Senate Foreign Relations Committee, which exercises life-and-death power over treaties, had been headed over a long period of years by Senators irrevocably committed to isolation, notably William E. Borah. Moreover, most observers of Senate action in the field of foreign affairs believe that the Executive has been inhibited again and again from taking bold and constructive action in cooperation with other nations by the fear that any agreements it might reach would be defeated in the Senate.

The President's lack of final authority in treaty-making, in turn, inhibits other nations from trusting any promises he may make.

Tug of War between Senate and Executive

The Executive's fear of the Senate, which in the past has been as automatic a reflex as the Senate's suspicion of the Executive when it comes to foreign affairs, has led successive Presidents to by-pass the Senate by casting international arrangements in two other forms: executive agreements, which do not need to be passed on by Congress, or joint resolutions, which require only approval by a majority of both the Senate and the House. The UNRRA agreement, for example, was submitted, and adopted, in the form of an executive agreement in 1944. The Senate, however, has become increasingly reluctant to allow subject matter which it believes belongs in treaties subject to its ratification to be embodied in executive agreements. In practice it is wellnigh impossible to decide which international matters belong properly in the category of treaties, and which in the category of executive agreements—although the suggestion has been made that arrangements that do not require the use of this country's military forces or financial resources might be placed in the latter category.

Actually, it is both undignified, and not straightforward, for the Executive to have to seek round-about ways of avoiding action by the Senate. But, unless reforms can be effected in the existing machinery of treaty-making, the country could be confronted with two equally undesirable alternatives. Either it would have to forego a policy of cooperation and follow a strictly lone-hand policy, which would call for a minimum of negotiations and agreements with other nations;

or else, if it decides that a policy of cooperation is essential to the national interest, then the President would either increasingly have to adopt a dictatorial tone toward Congress, or else he would be driven to conducting foreign policy literally "underground" in the hope of eventually enlisting public support for such decisions as he and his State Department advisers may take. The "underground" way of negotiating with other nations is not only unsatisfactory to those with whom we are negotiating, since they never have any assurance that the United States will finally abide by the decisions of the President and the State Department. It would also weaken and ultimately destroy the confidence of the voters, who would thus be deprived of any opportunity of participating in the making of this country's foreign policy.

Two Reforms Essential

True, President Truman appears to have overcome some of the difficulties encountered by his predecessors in dealing with the Senate on treaty-making. But it would be unwise to accept his success with respect to the Charter as a decisive precedent. For in the future other Presidents who might not be as intimately familiar with the members of the Senate or as attuned to their wishes as Mr. Truman might be confronted with the same problems that baffled Woodrow Wilson and the two Roosevelts.

What reforms might be made to alleviate these problems? Two measures that would greatly help the situation have long been under consideration. First, it has been proposed, through resolutions introduced in both the House and the Senate, that the Constitution should be amended in such a way as to provide for ratification of treaties by a simple majority of both houses of Congress. There are a number of reasons why it seems desirable that the House should participate in the making of foreign policy on an equal footing with the Senate—among them the fact that in recent years the House has seemed, on the whole, to reflect public opinion more accurately and more promptly than the Senate. It seems doubtful, however, that the Senate, jealous of its special prerogatives with respect to treaties, would look with favor on any proposal to share these prerogatives with the House.

But should it prove impossible to get resolutions to this effect through Congress, the next best method—and a vast improvement over the two-thirds rule—would be a constitutional amendment providing that treaties shall be subject to approval by a simple majority of the Senate. Such an amendment, like all amendments to the Constitution, would have to be submitted to the legislatures of the forty-eight states, and the process, once set in motion, is expected to take at least two years. This, however, should not discourage supporters of the amendment from pressing for its discussion. The very fact that it is kept before the public during the crucial months of the post-war period will have at least an indirect effect on the Senate, one-third of whose membership was renewed in the 1944 elections, with notable additions to the ranks of Senators who favor a policy of cooperation with other nations—among them J. William Fulbright of Arkansas, Leverett Saltonstall of Massachusetts, H. Alexander Smith of New Jersey, Wayne Morse of Oregon, and others.

The second measure proposed to improve the existing machinery for shaping United States foreign policy is to establish continuous consultation on current negotiations between the Executive and Congress. Such consultation would become urgently necessary, in fact, if both the Senate and the House should be charged with the responsibility of approving treaties, since both houses would then require information from the Executive on the background of treaties submitted to them. There is at present no method by which members of the Senate are regularly informed concerning the problems of our foreign relations daily faced by the President and the State Department. The consequence is that often when the Senate does finally receive a treaty or agreement of whose initial stages it is ignorant, it feels that it has been confronted by a *fait accompli* and balks at accepting it—whereas if it had been informed at all stages of the difficulties encountered, the compromises reached, the gains achieved, it might adopt an entirely different attitude. Former Secretary of State Hull did acquaint members of the Senate Foreign Relations Committee with certain important negotiations, notably the Moscow conference and the Dumbarton Oaks proposals; and the inclusion of members of the Senate in the United States delegation to Mexico City and San Francisco marked a significant step in the direction of cooperation between the Executive and Congress in treaty-making. In the future, however, it would be desirable to establish a permanent channel for the presentation of information on international relations by the Executive to Congress, so that whenever it is necessary to implement the good-neighbor intentions of the American people by concrete measures, Congress cannot plead ignorance and the Executive cannot plead Congressional non-cooperation as an excuse for inaction.

But the foreign policy of the United States is determined not only by the Executive and Congress. There is a third and by no means silent partner in the difficult enterprise of shaping our relations with other nations. That third partner is yourself, in your capacity as voter. It is what our citizens think and say that makes up what we call public opinion. Under our system of government, the President and Congress must constantly scrutinize and weigh public opinion if they are not to march too far ahead or fall too far behind the prevailing views of the people. In the making of foreign policy, particularly, the President must be fairly certain that he can carry with him a majority of the voters if he is to persuade other countries that the statements he issues or the treaties the State Department negotiates represent public opinion in this country and will be supported by the people. Otherwise his voice, even though it be the voice of a prophet ahead of his time, as was that of Woodrow Wilson in 1919, will be a voice in the wilderness.

Our Varied Background and Foreign Policy

It is no easy task to determine at any given moment just what is public opinion on current issues of foreign affairs. Ours is a nation built up by immigrants from many lands on all continents, some of whom came as early as the sixteenth century and some as late as the 1930's. Many of us retain sentimental attachments to the nations where we or our parents or grandparents were born, even though we may have no desire whatever to live there. Just as Americans of English origin have a specially warm place in their heart for England, so people who stem from Germany or the Scandinavian countries or Poland or Russia bear somewhere within them the imprint of the lands where they were born or whose traditions have been woven into their lives. This makes us react more promptly and strongly to events outside our borders than is true of peoples like the British or French, who for centuries have lived together and have relatively few ties of blood with other continents.

Because of this situation, any issue of foreign policy is apt to be judged here not only in terms of how it affects or might be affected by the United States, but also of the impact it has on the particular country involved. Citizens of Polish origin, for example, have expressed strong views concerning the Russo-Polish controversy; citizens of Finnish background enlisted American sympathies on the side of Finland against Russia in 1939-40; citizens of Serb and Croat descent have clashed here during the struggle between their respective peoples in Yugoslavia. However, their concern about affairs in their overseas homelands did not diminish their loyalty to the United States, which was abundantly proved every day during two world wars. In fact, by a strange paradox, many of our citizens of European origin, while full of sympathy for the troubles suffered by their homelands, often are by no means anxious to have the United States intervene abroad. "We (or our forefathers)," they say, "fled from tyranny and poverty in these countries to the haven of the Promised Land over here, and we don't want to get mixed up again in the very turmoils and conflicts we had hoped to leave behind us forever." Yet no political leader in this country can disregard the possibility, especially when election day comes, that this decision or that in foreign policy may lose him the Polish vote or the Italian vote. This peculiar feature of American political life will become gradually less important as time goes on, and more and more of our citizens concentrate all their attention and sentiments on the building of the United States.

Ideals in International Affairs

Meanwhile, our concern for other countries is due not so much to the sentimental attachment of our citizens to their homelands as to a strong sense of idealism which is our common heritage of American traditions. This idealism causes us again and again to feel shocked by injuries inflicted on other peoples, to demand freedom and justice for all, and to seek ways of performing acts of kindness and mercy abroad. George Washington expressed this profound aspiration of the American people when he said, in his Farewell Address: "It will be worthy of a free, enlightened, and at no distant period, a great nation to give to mankind the magnanimous and too novel example of a people always guided by an exalted justice and benevolence."

This, we would all agree, is a most praiseworthy goal for us to pursue. However, sometimes the United States has fallen short of its own ideals, as all human societies are bound to do. Yet we often discuss international affairs as if this country alone has ideals, as if all other nations act solely from sordid motives. As President Roosevelt said in his 1945 message to Congress on the state of the Union, it is dangerous for any nation to claim a monopoly of virtue. Other nations, too, have ideals. But sometimes an unfortunate geographic position, or poor economic resources, or inadequate political leadership make it difficult for them to transform ideals into practice.

We must constantly be on the watch for what is in international relations our greatest national weakness—our tendency to think that we have done our share if we just proclaim our ideals and then let other peoples do the dirty work of carrying them out, while we look on as interested but irresponsible spectators, cheering some, admonishing others, but never taking an active part ourselves in the difficult and never-ending task of translating ideals into reality. Ideals that are never put to work are like idle capital: they benefit no one, not even the idealist.

The time has come when we, as a nation, must step down from the lofty pedestal we have occupied since the foundation of this nation into what an English periodical has called "the dust of the arena." Then we shall begin to see the difficulties that arise when we ourselves work with other nations to put ideals into effect, and we may become more tolerant of our neighbors. The policy we have followed until now can be described as a policy of intermittent intervention abroad at such times and under such circumstances as we ourselves determined. From now on we cannot shrink from the political and economic responsibilities of our military operations in Europe and Asia. This will mean that the United States will no longer be able to rely on "temporary alliances for extraordinary emergencies," as George Washington proposed in an age whose problems differed vastly from ours, and as we have done in two world wars, but will have to assume lasting commitments as an active participant in an international organization.

What Can the Voter Expect from Government?

Now that the United States is on the point of expanding its collaboration with other nations, what can you as a voter expect to obtain from the government to assist you in making up your mind on issues of foreign affairs? The voter can reasonably ask two things. First, he can ask that the State Department be more promptly responsive than in the past to currents of public opinion. Changes in the internal organization of the State Department effected during 1944 —such as the reshuffling of various existing posts and the creation of new ones, notably on labor problems—and the need, forced by the exigencies of war, to recruit personnel on a broader basis, are steps in the right direction. It is essential, however, that members of the State Department, many of whom must spend years abroad in foreign service, should have an opportunity to be in touch as closely as possible with the rough-and-tumble of national life, with the hopes and fears of their fellow-citizens, so that they can bear in mind American conditions and preferences when they negotiate with other nations.

The voter can also ask for more information about current international negotiations—not, of course, about the details of day-to-day conversations with representatives of other nations, which must necessarily enjoy a measure of privacy, but about the objectives the government is seeking to achieve and the methods it is using to achieve them. It is true that in the past—especially during the critical years that preceded the outbreak of World War II—the President and various government officials did make statements on foreign affairs. But these statements, coming at irregular intervals, and often in disconnected fashion, did not seem to catch the attention of the people. During the war the voters were often left without official information for long periods of time on such crucial questions as our relations with Franco Spain, our attitude toward de Gaulle, and our plans for the future of Germany, which were matters of vigorous public debate. Some method of maintaining a continuous flow of forthright information to the public must be devised by the State Department if we are to fulfill Mr. Hull's ideal that "the people, who are sovereign, must not only educate their servants but must be willing to be educated by them." The interest shown by former Secretary of State Stettinius in the need of improving the department's public information services gives promise that further reforms may be undertaken in this field.

What the Voter Can Do

Yet it is not enough for voters to know about foreign affairs. They must also have an opportunity to put their knowledge to work by conveying their views, again with some measure of continuity, to the Executive. In theory they should be able to do this by electing to Congress Representatives and Senators who can speak for them not only on domestic but also on foreign affairs, and by maintaining a constant watch on the opinions expressed and actions taken by their elected spokesmen. For a variety of reasons, however, the people have not always been able to make full use of their opportunity to shape the views of Congress on foreign affairs. Elections are fought usually on domestic rather than on foreign policy issues, and local considerations have a profound influence on the selection of Congressmen. Yet again and again in recent years unofficial observers have had the impression that the people, at least the articulate elements, were way ahead of many Congressmen in their grasp of foreign affairs and in their readiness to consider post-war plans.

If this is true, then there is a dangerous gulf between Congress and the public on foreign policy—a gulf that must be bridged. One of our difficulties is that on many crucial issues—for example, whether or not the country should join the League of Nations—foreign policy has been finally determined by relatively small but strongly organized groups.

These could bring to bear on congressmen the kind of per-suasive pressure that the average, unorganized citizen is usu-ally not in a position to exert. From now on it is imperative that the voters should be constantly on the alert to detect the influence that self-seeking pressure groups exercise on the conduct of foreign policy, and they should counteract it by equally well-planned and well-directed political action.

What forms can this action take? Some voters have a helpless, frustrated feeling that they can do nothing unless they are in the seats of the mighty in Washington. This is wrong. There are certain things that every voter can do about foreign policy without leaving his or her home town, and some even without leaving home. Every voter should be familiar with what is being taught to our children in schools and colleges about international relations. If we think that the materials taught are not true to facts, or are distorted by bias, we should take up the matter with our school boards and teachers. Every voter should follow the presentation of news, and especially editorials on foreign affairs, in the local newspaper, and by letters to the editor, or direct appeal to the publisher, counteract falsification or prejudice. Every voter should urge the local radio station to carry, as is done in some communities, daily or weekly accounts of what congressmen from that area are doing about international affairs. Every voter can take part in the various groups now in existence for study or action, or both, in the field of foreign policy, or help to form new ones. Every voter can share in the local activities of the political party to which he or she belongs and see to it that the party organization is interested not only in local problems, but also in problems of foreign affairs.

Even those who are not yet of voting age can, as students

in high school or college, prepare themselves for the tasks of citizenship in a democratic nation whose sense of responsibility will determine the success of international organization. All students can study with special concern the history, geography, economy, and culture not only of this country, but also of other countries, and talk things over with fellow students, teachers, and parents. They can make whatever group they belong to—Boy or Girl Scouts, 4-H Clubs, student government associations—centers of thought and discussion about this country's position in the modern world. Nothing the individual does is too small to count. It must always be remembered that no successful human institution was built in one day, and that each of us can contribute to the building of world order as we go through life.

Once Congress, through the reforms previously suggested, has become closely meshed with the Executive in the formulation and execution of foreign policy, and citizens have acquired both knowledge of foreign affairs and developed the willingness to exercise their privileges as voters, our nation will be in a far stronger position than in the past to match words with deeds, and to act responsibly in the United Nations organization. For far too long voters have felt that their main concern was with local affairs, or at best with national domestic affairs, and that foreign affairs were the concern of the President, the State Department, and a few commentators. Now we have all discovered, through the most bitter experience, that foreign affairs are a matter of life and death for every one of us. They should remain a matter of life and death even when the war is over. If we fail to see to this, we shall be betraying by default the privileges of citizenship in a democratic society for which millions of people, including our own, have died in two wars.

As a young aviator from Connecticut, killed overseas, wrote: "If the country takes these sacrifices with indifference, it will be the cruelest ingratitude the world has ever known. You will, I know, do all in your power to help others keep faith with those few who gave so much."

TEXTS OF DOCUMENTS

DUMBARTON OAKS DOCUMENTS ON INTERNATIONAL ORGANIZATION *

STATEMENT BY THE PRESIDENT OF THE UNITED STATES REGARDING THE DUMBARTON OAKS PROPOSALS

I WISH to take this opportunity to refer to the work of the Dumbarton Oaks Conversations between the delegations of the United States, the United Kingdom, the Soviet Union, and China on the plans for an international organization for the maintenance of peace and security.

The conversations were completed Saturday, October 7, 1944, and proposals were submitted to the four Governments for their consideration. These proposals have been made public to permit full discussion by the people of this country prior to the convening of a wider conference on this all-important subject.

Although I have not yet been able to make a thorough study of these proposals, my first impression is one of extreme satisfaction, and even surprise, that so much could have been accomplished on so difficult a subject in so short a time. This achievement was largely due to the long and thorough preparations which were made by the Governments represented, and in our case, was the result of the untiring devotion and care which the Secretary of State has

* Department of State, Publication 2192, Conference Series 56.

personally given to this work for more than two and a half years—indeed for many years.

The projected international organization has for its primary purpose the maintenance of international peace and security and the creation of the conditions that make for peace.

We now know the need for such an organization of the peace-loving peoples and the spirit of unity which will be required to maintain it. Aggressors like Hitler and the Japanese war lords organize for years for the day when they can launch their evil strength against weaker nations devoted to their peaceful pursuits. This time we have been determined first to defeat the enemy, assure that he shall never again be in position to plunge the world into war, and then to so organize the peace-loving nations that they may through unity of desire, unity of will, and unity of strength be in position to assure that no other would-be aggressor or conqueror shall even get started. That is why from the very beginning of the war, and paralleling our military plans, we have begun to lay the foundations for the general organization for the maintenance of peace and security.

It represents, therefore, a major objective for which this war is being fought, and as such, it inspires the highest hopes of the millions of fathers and mothers whose sons and daughters are engaged in the terrible struggle and suffering of war.

The projected general organization may be regarded as the keystone of the arch and will include within its framework a number of specialized economic and social agencies now existing or to be established.

The task of planning the great design of security and peace has been well begun. It now remains for the nations to complete the structure in a spirit of constructive purpose and mutual confidence.

OCTOBER 9, 1944

STATEMENT BY THE SECRETARY OF STATE OF THE UNITED STATES

The proposals for an international organization for the maintenance of international peace and security, upon which the representatives of the United States, the United Kingdom, the Soviet Union, and China have agreed during the conversations at Dumbarton Oaks, have been submitted to the four Governments and are today being made generally available to the people of this Nation and of the world.

All of us have every reason to be immensely gratified by the results achieved at these conversations. To be sure, the Proposals in their present form are neither complete nor final. Much work still remains to be done before a set of completed proposals can be placed before the peace-loving nations of the world as a basis of discussion at a formal conference to draft a charter of the projected organization for submission to the governments. But the document which has been prepared by the able representatives of the four participating nations and has been agreed to by them as their recommendation to their respective Governments is sufficiently detailed to indicate the kind of an international organization which, in their judgment, will meet the imperative need of providing for the maintenance of international peace and security.

These proposals are now being studied by the four Governments which were represented at the Washington Conversations and which will give their urgent attention to the next steps which will be necessary to reach the goal of achieving the establishment of an effective international organization.

These proposals are now available for full study and discussion by the peoples of all countries.

We in this country have spent many months in careful planning and wide consultation in preparation for the conversations which have just been concluded. Those who represented the Government of the United States in these discussions were armed with the ideas and with the results of thinking contributed by numerous leaders of our national thought and opinion, without regard to political or other affiliations.

It is my earnest hope that, during the time which must elapse before the convocation of a full United Nations conference, discussions in the United States on this all-important subject will continue to be carried on in the same nonpartisan spirit of devotion to our paramount national interest in peace and security which has characterized our previous consultations. I am certain that all of us will be constantly mindful of the high responsibility for us and for all peace-loving nations which attaches to this effort to make permanent a victory purchased at so heavy a cost in blood, in tragic suffering, and in treasure. We must be constantly mindful of the price which all of us will pay if we fail to measure up to this unprecedented responsibility.

It is, of course, inevitable that when many governments and peoples attempt to agree on a single plan the result will be in terms of the highest common denominator rather than of the plan of any one nation. The organization to be created must reflect the ideas and hopes of all the peace-loving nations which participate in its creation. The spirit of co-operation must manifest itself in mutual striving to attain the high goal by common agreement.

The road to the establishment of an international organization capable of effectively maintaining international peace and security will be long. At times it will be difficult. But we cannot hope to attain so great an objective without constant effort and unfailing determination that the sacrifices of this war shall not be in vain.

OCTOBER 9, 1944

REPORT TO THE SECRETARY OF STATE

SUBMITTED BY THE CHAIRMAN OF THE AMERICAN DELEGATION TO THE WASHINGTON CONVERSATIONS ON INTERNATIONAL ORGANIZATION

I take great pleasure in submitting to you the results of the exploratory conversations on international organization held in Washington between representatives of the Governments of the United States, the United Kingdom, the Soviet Union, and China. The first phase of the conversations, between representatives of the United States, the United Kingdom, and the Soviet Union, took place from August 21 to September 28; the second phase, between representatives of the United States, the United Kingdom, and China, was held from September 29 to October 7. The results of the work accomplished in both phases are embodied in the following Proposals which each of the four delegations is transmitting to its respective Government as the unanimously agreed recommendations of the four delegations.

I am happy to report that the conversations throughout

were characterized by a spirit of complete cooperation and great cordiality among all participants, the proof of which is evident in the wide area of agreement covered in the Proposals. The few questions which remain for further consideration, though important, are not in any sense insuperable, and I recommend that the necessary steps for obtaining agreement on these points be taken as soon as possible.

It is proper to emphasize, at the conclusion of these preliminary conversations, that the Proposals as they are now submitted to the four Governments comprise substantial contributions from each of the delegations. It is my own view, which I believe is shared by all the participants, that the agreed Proposals constitute an advance over the tentative and preliminary proposals presented by each delegation. This has resulted from a single-minded effort of all the delegations at Dumbarton Oaks to reach a common understanding as to the most effective international organization capable of fulfilling the hopes of all peoples everywhere.

I wish to take this opportunity to express my grateful recognition of the contribution to the successful outcome of these conversations made by the members of the American delegation and to commend the advisers and the staff for their most helpful assistance. Above all, I wish to express my profound appreciation to the President and to you, Mr. Secretary, for the constant advice and guidance without which our work could not have been accomplished with such constructive and satisfactory results.

E. R. STETTINIUS, JR.

OCTOBER 7, 1944

STATEMENT ISSUED SIMULTANEOUSLY BY THE PARTICIPATING GOVERNMENTS

The Government of the United States has now received the report of its delegation to the conversations held in Washington between August 21 and October 7, 1944, with the delegations of the United Kingdom, the Union of Soviet Socialist Republics, and the Republic of China on the subject of an international organization for the maintenance of peace and security.

There follows a statement of tentative proposals indicating in detail the wide range of subjects on which agreement has been reached at the conversations.

The Governments which were represented in the discussions in Washington have agreed that after further study of these proposals they will as soon as possible take the necessary steps with a view to the preparation of complete proposals which could then serve as a basis of discussion at a full United Nations conference.

OCTOBER 9, 1944

PROPOSALS FOR THE ESTABLISHMENT OF A GENERAL INTERNATIONAL ORGANIZATION

(DUMBARTON OAKS PROPOSALS)

There should be established an international organization under the title of The United Nations, the Charter of which should contain provisions necessary to give effect to the proposals which follow.

Chapter I. Purposes

The purposes of the Organization should be:

1. To maintain international peace and security; and to that end to take effective collective measures for the prevention and removal of threats to the peace and the suppression of acts of aggression or other breaches of the peace, and to bring about by peaceful means adjustment or settlement of international disputes which may lead to a breach of the peace;

2. To develop friendly relations among nations and to take other appropriate measures to strengthen universal peace;

3. To achieve international cooperation in the solution of international economic, social and other humanitarian problems; and

4. To afford a center for harmonizing the actions of nations in the achievement of these common ends.

Chapter II. Principles

In pursuit of the purposes mentioned in Chapter I the Organization and its members should act in accordance with the following principles:

1. The Organization is based on the principle of the sovereign equality of all peace-loving states.

2. All members of the Organization undertake, in order to ensure to all of them the rights and benefits resulting from membership in the Organization, to fulfill the obligations assumed by them in accordance with the Charter.

3. All members of the Organization shall settle their disputes by peaceful means in such a manner that international peace and security are not endangered.

4. All members of the Organization shall refrain in their international relations from the threat or use of force in any manner inconsistent with the purposes of the Organization.

5. All members of the Organization shall give every assistance to the Organization in any action undertaken by it in accordance with the provisions of the Charter.

6. All members of the Organization shall refrain from giving assistance to any state against which preventive or enforcement action is being undertaken by the Organization.

The Organization should ensure that states not members of the Organization act in accordance with these principles so far as may be necessary for the maintenance of international peace and security.

Chapter III. Membership

1. Membership of the Organization should be open to all peace-loving states.

Chapter IV. Principal Organs

1. The Organization should have as its principal organs:
    a. A General Assembly;
    b. A Security Council;
    c. An international court of justice; and
    d. A Secretariat.

2. The Organization should have such subsidiary agencies as may be found necessary.

Chapter V. The General Assembly

Section A. Composition

All members of the Organization should be members of the General Assembly and should have a number of representatives to be specified in the Charter.

Section B. Functions and Powers

1. The General Assembly should have the right to consider the general principles of cooperation in the maintenance of international peace and security, including the principles governing disarmament and the regulation of armaments; to discuss any questions relating to the maintenance of international peace and security brought before it by any member or members of the Organization or by the Security Council; and to make recommendations with regard to any such principles or questions. Any such questions on which action is necessary should be referred to the Security Council by the General Assembly either before or after discussion. The General Assembly should not on its own initiative make recommendations on any matter relating to the maintenance of international peace and security which is being dealt with by the Security Council.

2. The General Assembly should be empowered to admit new members to the Organization upon recommendation of the Security Council.

3. The General Assembly should, upon recommendation of the Security Council, be empowered to suspend from the exercise of any rights or privileges of membership any member of the Organization against which preventive or enforcement action shall have been taken by the Security Council. The exercise of the rights and privileges thus suspended may be restored by decision of the Security Council. The General Assembly should be empowered, upon recommendation of the Security Council, to expel from the Organization any member of the Organization which persistently violates the principles contained in the Charter.

4. The General Assembly should elect the non-permanent

members of the Security Council and the members of the Economic and Social Council provided for in Chapter IX. It should be empowered to elect, upon recommendation of the Security Council, the Secretary-General of the Organization. It should perform such functions in relation to the election of the judges of the international court of justice as may be conferred upon it by the statute of the court.

5. The General Assembly should apportion the expenses among the members of the Organization and should be empowered to approve the budgets of the Organization.

6. The General Assembly should initiate studies and make recommendations for the purpose of promoting international cooperation in political, economic and social fields and of adjusting situations likely to impair the general welfare.

7. The General Assembly should make recommendations for the coordination of the policies of international economic, social, and other specialized agencies brought into relation with the Organization in accordance with agreements between such agencies and the Organization.

8. The General Assembly should receive and consider annual and special reports from the Security Council and reports from other bodies of the Organization.

Section C. Voting

1. Each member of the Organization should have one vote in the General Assembly.

2. Important decisions of the General Assembly, including recommendations with respect to the maintenance of international peace and security; election of members of the Security Council; election of members of the Economic and Social Council; admission of members, suspension of the

exercise of the rights and privileges of members, and expulsion of members; and budgetary questions, should be made by a two-thirds majority of those present and voting. On other questions, including the determination of additional categories of questions to be decided by a two-thirds majority, the decisions of the General Assembly should be made by a simple majority vote.

Section D. Procedure

1. The General Assembly should meet in regular annual sessions and in such special sessions as occasion may require.

2. The General Assembly should adopt its own rules of procedure and elect its President for each session.

3. The General Assembly should be empowered to set up such bodies and agencies as it may deem necessary for the performance of its functions.

CHAPTER VI. THE SECURITY COUNCIL

Section A. Composition

The Security Council should consist of one representative of each of eleven members of the Organization. Representatives of the United States of America, the United Kingdom of Great Britain and Northern Ireland, the Union of Soviet Socialist Republics, the Republic of China, and, in due course, France, should have permanent seats. The General Assembly should elect six states to fill the non-permanent seats. These six states should be elected for a term of two year, three retiring each year. They should not be immediately eligible for reelection. In the first election of the non-permanent members three should be chosen by the General Assembly for one-year terms and three for two-year terms.

Section B. Principal Functions and Powers

1. In order to ensure prompt and effective action by the Organization, members of the Organization should by the Charter confer on the Security Council primary responsibility for the maintenance of international peace and security and should agree that in carrying out these duties under this responsibility it should act on their behalf.

2. In discharging these duties the Security Council should act in accordance with the purposes and principles of the Organization.

3. The specific powers conferred on the Security Council in order to carry out these duties are laid down in Chapter VIII.

4. All members of the Organization should obligate themselves to accept the decisions of the Security Council and to carry them out in accordance with the provisions of the Charter.

5. In order to promote the establishment and maintenance of international peace and security with the least diversion of the world's human and economic resources for armaments, the Security Council, with the assistance of the Military Staff Committee referred to in Chapter VIII, Section B, paragraph 9, should have the responsibility for formulating plans for the establishment of a system of regulation of armaments for submission to the members of the Organization.

Section C. Voting

(NOTE.—The question of voting procedure in the Security Council is still under consideration.)

Section D. Procedure

1. The Security Council should be so organized as to be able to function continuously and each state member of the Security Council should be permanently represented at the headquarters of the Organization. It may hold meetings at such other places as in its judgment may best facilitate its work. There should be periodic meetings at which each state member of the Security Council could if it so desired be represented by a member of the government or some other special representative.

2. The Security Council should be empowered to set up such bodies or agencies as it may deem necessary for the performance of its functions including regional subcommittees of the Military Staff Committee.

3. The Security Council should adopt its own rules of procedure, including the method of selecting its President.

4. Any member of the Organization should participate in the discussion of any question brought before the Security Council whenever the Security Council considers that the interests of that member of the Organization are specially affected.

5. Any member of the Organization not having a seat on the Security Council and any state not a member of the Organization, if it is a party to a dispute under consideration by the Security Council, should be invited to participate in the discussion relating to the dispute.

Chapter VII. An International Court of Justice

1. There should be an international court of justice which should constitute the principal judicial organ of the Organization.

2. The court should be constituted and should function in accordance with a statute which should be annexed to and be a part of the Charter of the Organization.

3. The statute of the court of international justice should be either (a) the Statute of the Permanent Court of International Justice, continued in force with such modifications as may be desirable or (b) a new statute in the preparation of which the Statute of the Permanent Court of International Justice should be used as a basis.

4. All members of the Organization should *ipso facto* be parties to the statute of the international court of justice.

5. Conditions under which states not members of the Organization may become parties to the statute of the international court of justice should be determined in each case by the General Assembly upon recommendation of the Security Council.

CHAPTER VIII. ARRANGEMENTS FOR THE MAINTENANCE OF INTERNATIONAL PEACE AND SECURITY INCLUDING PREVENTION AND SUPPRESSION OF AGGRESSION

Section A. Pacific Settlement of Disputes

1. The Security Council should be empowered to investigate any dispute, or any situation which may lead to international friction or give rise to a dispute, in order to determine whether its continuance is likely to endanger the maintenance of international peace and security.

2. Any state, whether member of the Organization or not, may bring any such dispute or situation to the attention of the General Assembly or of the Security Council.

3. The parties to any dispute the continuance of which is likely to endanger the maintenance of international peace and security should obligate themselves, first of all, to seek

a solution by negotiation, mediation, conciliation, arbitration or judicial settlement, or other peaceful means of their own choice. The Security Council should call upon the parties to settle their dispute by such means.

4. If, nevertheless, parties to a dispute of the nature referred to in paragraph 3 above fail to settle it by the means indicated in that paragraph, they should obligate themselves to refer it to the Security Council. The Security Council should in each case decide whether or not the continuance of the particular dispute is in fact likely to endanger the maintenance of international peace and security, and, accordingly, whether the Security Council should deal with the dispute, and, if so, whether it should take action under paragraph 5.

5. The Security Council should be empowered, at any stage of a dispute of the nature referred to in paragraph 3 above, to recommend appropriate procedures or methods of adjustment.

6. Justiciable disputes should normally be referred to the international court of justice. The Security Council should be empowered to refer to the court, for advice, legal questions connected with other disputes.

7. The provisions of paragraph 1 to 6 of Section A should not apply to situations or disputes arising out of matters which by international law are solely within the domestic jurisdiction of the state concerned.

Section B. Determination of Threats to the Peace or Acts of Aggression and Action with Respect Thereto

1. Should the Security Council deem that a failure to settle a dispute in accordance with procedures indicated in paragraph 3 of Section A, or in accordance with its recom-

mendations made under paragraph 5 of Section A, constitutes a threat to the maintenance of international peace and security, it should take any measures necessary for the maintenance of international peace and security in accordance with the purposes and principles of the Organization.

2. In general the Security Council should determine the existence of any threat to the peace, breach of the peace or act of aggression and should make recommendations or decide upon the measures to be taken to maintain or restore peace and security.

3. The Security Council should be empowered to determine what diplomatic, economic, or other measures not involving the use of armed force should be employed to give effect to its decisions, and to call upon members of the Organization to apply such measures. Such measures may include complete or partial interruption of rail, sea, air, postal, telegraphic, radio and other means of communication and the severance of diplomatic and economic relations.

4. Should the Security Council consider such measures to be inadequate, it should be empowered to take such action by air, naval or land forces as may be necessary to maintain or restore international peace and security. Such action may include demonstrations, blockade and other operations by air, sea or land forces of members of the Organization.

5. In order that all members of the Organization should contribute to the maintenance of international peace and security, they should undertake to make available to the Security Council, on its call and in accordance with a special agreement or agreements concluded among themselves, armed forces, facilities and assistance necessary for the purpose of maintaining international peace and security. Such agreement or agreements should govern the numbers and types of

forces and the nature of the facilities and assistance to be provided. The special agreement or agreements should be negotiated as soon as possible and should in each case be subject to approval by the Security Council and to ratification by the signatory states in accordance with their constitutional processes.

6. In order to enable urgent military measures to be taken by the Organization there should be held immediately available by the members of the Organization national air force contingents for combined international enforcement action. The strength and degree of readiness of these contingents and plans for their combined action should be determined by the Security Council with the assistance of the Military Staff Committee within the limits laid down in the special agreement or agreements referred to in paragraph 5 above.

7. The action required to carry out the decisions of the Security Council for the maintenance of international peace and security should be taken by all the members of the Organization in cooperation or by some of them as the Security Council may determine. This undertaking should be carried out by the members of the Organization by their own action and through action of the appropriate specialized organizations and agencies of which they are members.

8. Plans for the application of armed force should be made by the Security Council with the assistance of the Military Staff Committee referred to in paragraph 9 below.

9. There should be established a Military Staff Committee the functions of which should be to advise and assist the Security Council on all questions relating to the Security Council's military requirements for the maintenance of international peace and security, to the employment and com-

mand of forces placed at its disposal, to the regulation of armaments, and to possible disarmament. It should be responsible under the Security Council for the strategic direction of any armed forces placed at the disposal of the Security Council. The Committee should be composed of the Chiefs of Staff of the permanent members of the Security Council or their representatives. Any member of the Organization not permanently represented on the Committee should be invited by the Committee to be associated with it when the efficient discharge of the Committee's responsibilities requires that such a state should participate in its work. Questions of command of forces should be worked out subsequently.

10. The members of the Organization should join in affording mutual assistance in carrying out the measures decided upon by the Security Council.

11. Any state, whether a member of the Organization or not, which finds itself confronted with special economic problems arising from the carrying out of measures which have been decided upon by the Security Council should have the right to consult the Security Council in regard to a solution of those problems.

Section C. Regional Arrangements

1. Nothing in the Charter should preclude the existence of regional arrangements or agencies for dealing with such matters relating to the maintenance of international peace and security as are appropriate for regional action, provided such arrangements or agencies and their activities are consistent with the purposes and principles of the Organization. The Security Council should encourage settlement of local disputes through such regional arrangements or by such

regional agencies, either on the initiative of the states concerned or by reference from the Security Council.

2. The Security Council should, where appropriate, utilize such arrangements or agencies for enforcement action under its authority, but no enforcement action should be taken under regional arrangements or by regional agencies without the authorization of the Security Council.

3. The Security Council should at all times be kept fully informed of activities undertaken or in contemplation under regional arrangements or by regional agencies for the maintenance of international peace and security.

CHAPTER IX. ARRANGEMENTS FOR INTERNATIONAL ECONOMIC AND SOCIAL COOPERATION

Section A. Purpose and Relationships

1. With a view to the creation of conditions of stability and well-being which are necessary for peaceful and friendly relations among nations, the Organization should facilitate solutions of international economic, social and other humanitarian problems and promote respect for human rights and fundamental freedoms. Responsibility for the discharge of this function should be vested in the General Assembly and, under the authority of the General Assembly, in an Economic and Social Council.

2. The various specialized economic, social and other organizations and agencies would have responsibilities in their respective fields as defined in their statutes. Each such organization or agency should be brought into relationship with the Organization on terms to be determined by agreement between the Economic and Social Council and the appropriate authorities of the specialized organization or agency, subject to approval by the General Assembly.

Section B. Composition and Voting

The Economic and Social Council should consist of representatives of eighteen members of the Organization. The states to be represented for this purpose should be elected by the General Assembly for terms of three years. Each such state should have one representative, who should have one vote. Decisions of the Economic and Social Council should be taken by simple majority vote of those present and voting.

Section C. Functions and Powers of the Economic and Social Council

1. The Economic and Social Council should be empowered:

    a. to carry out, within the scope of its functions, recommendations of the General Assembly;

    b. to make recommendations, on its own initiative, with respect to international economic, social and other humanitarian matters;

    c. to receive and consider reports from the economic, social and other organizations or agencies brought into relationship with the Organization, and to coordinate their activities through consultations with, and recommendations to, such organizations or agencies;

    d. to examine the administrative budgets of such specialized organizations or agencies with a view to making recommendations to the organizations or agencies concerned;

    e. to enable the Secretary-General to provide information to the Security Council;

f. to assist the Security Council upon its request; and

g. to perform such other functions within the general scope of its competence as may be assigned to it by the General Assembly.

Section D. Organization and Procedure

1. The Economic and Social Council should set up an economic commission, a social commission, and such other commissions as may be required. These commissions should consist of experts. There should be a permanent staff which should constitute a part of the Secretariat of the Organization.

2. The Economic and Social Council should make suitable arrangements for representatives of the specialized organizations or agencies to participate without vote in its deliberations and in those of the commissions established by it.

3. The Economic and Social Council should adopt its own rules of procedure and the method of selecting its President.

CHAPTER X. THE SECRETARIAT

1. There should be a Secretariat comprising a Secretary-General and such staff as may be required. The Secretary-General should be the chief administrative officer of the Organization. He should be elected by the General Assembly, on recommendation of the Security Council, for such term and under such conditions as are specified in the Charter.

2. The Secretary-General should act in that capacity in all meetings of the General Assembly, of the Security Council, and of the Economic and Social Council and should make an annual report to the General Assembly on the work of the Organization.

3. The Secretary-General should have the right to bring to the attention of the Security Council any matter which in his opinion may threaten international peace and security.

Chapter XI. Amendments

Amendments should come into force for all members of the Organization, when they have been adopted by a vote of two-thirds of the members of the General Assembly and ratified in accordance with their respective constitutional processes by the members of the Organization having permanent membership on the Security Council and by a majority of the other members of the Organization.

Chapter XII. Transitional Arrangements

1. Pending the coming into force of the special agreement or agreements referred to in Chapter VIII, Section B, paragraph 5, and in accordance with the provisions of paragraph 5 of the Four-Nation Declaration, signed at Moscow, October 30, 1943, the states parties to that Declaration should consult with one another and as occasion arises with other members of the Organization with a view to such joint action on behalf of the Organization as may be necessary for the purpose of maintaining international peace and security.

2. No provision of the Charter should preclude action taken or authorized in relation to enemy states as a result of the present war by the Governments having responsibility for such action.

Note

In addition to the question of voting procedure in the Security Council referred to in Chapter VI, several other questions are still under consideration.

Washington, D. C.
October 7, 1944

THE CRIMEA CONFERENCE *

REPORT OF THE CONFERENCE

FOR the past eight days, Winston S. Churchill, Prime Minister of Great Britain, Franklin D. Roosevelt, President of the United States of America, and Marshal J. V. Stalin, Chairman of the Council of People's Commissars of the Union of Soviet Socialist Republics, have met with the Foreign Secretaries, Chiefs of Staff, and other advisers in the Crimea.

In addition to the three heads of government, the following took part in the conference:

For the United States of America

Edward R. Stettinius, Jr., Secretary of State

Fleet Admiral William D. Leahy, U.S.N., Chief of Staff to the President

Harry L. Hopkins, Special Assistant to the President

Justice James F. Byrnes, Director, Office of War Mobilization and Reconversion

General of the Army George C. Marshall, U.S.A., Chief of Staff, U. S. Army

Fleet Admiral Ernest J. King, U.S.N., Chief of Naval Operations and Commander in Chief, U. S. Fleet

Lieutenant General Brehon B. Somervell, Commanding General, Army Service Forces

Vice Admiral Emory S. Land, War Shipping Administrator

Major General L. S. Kuter, U.S.A., Staff of Commanding General, U. S. Army Air Forces

* Department of State, *Bulletin*, February 18, 1945, p. 213.

W. Averell Harriman, Ambassador to the U.S.S.R.

H. Freeman Matthews, Director, Office of European Affairs, State Department

Alger Hiss, Deputy Director, Office of Special Political Affairs, Department of State

Charles E. Bohlen, Assistant to the Secretary of State

together with political, military, and technical advisers.

For the United Kingdom

Anthony Eden, Secretary of State for Foreign Affairs

Lord Leathers, Minister of War Transport

Sir A. Clark-Kerr, H.M. Ambassador at Moscow

Sir Alexander Cadogan, Permanent Under Secretary of State for Foreign Affairs

Sir Edward Bridges, Secretary of the War Cabinet

Field Marshal Sir Alan Brooke, Chief of the Imperial General Staff

Marshal of the Royal Air Force Sir Charles Portal, Chief of the Air Staff

Admiral of the Fleet Sir Andrew Cunningham, First Sea Lord

General Sir Hastings Ismay, Chief of Staff to the Minister of Defense

together with

Field Marshal Alexander, Supreme Allied Commander, Mediterranean Theatre

Field Marshal Wilson, Head of the British Joint Staff Mission at Washington

Admiral Somerville, Joint Staff Mission at Washington

together with military and diplomatic advisers.

For the Soviet Union

V. M. Molotov, People's Commissar for Foreign Affairs of the U.S.S.R.

Admiral Kuznetsov, People's Commissar for the Navy

Army General Antonov, Deputy Chief of the General Staff of the Red Army

A. Y. Vyshinski, Deputy People's Commissar for Foreign Affairs of the U.S.S.R.

I. M. Maiski, Deputy People's Commissar of Foreign Affairs of the U.S.S.R.

Marshal of Aviation Khudyakov

F. T. Gusev, Ambassador in Great Britain

A. A. Gromyko, Ambassador in U.S.A.

The following statement is made by the Prime Minister of Great Britain, the President of the United States of America, and the Chairman of the Council of People's Commissars of the Union of Soviet Socialist Republics on the results of the Crimean Conference:

THE DEFEAT OF GERMANY

We have considered and determined the military plans of the three allied powers for the final defeat of the common enemy. The military staffs of the three allied nations have met in daily meetings throughout the Conference. These meetings have been most satisfactory from every point of view and have resulted in closer coordination of the military effort of the three allies than ever before. The fullest information has been interchanged. The timing, scope and coordination of new and even more powerful blows to be launched by our armies and air forces into the heart of Germany from the East, West, North and South have been fully agreed and planned in detail.

Our combined military plans will be made known only as we execute them, but we believe that the very close working partnership among the three staffs attained at this Conference will result in shortening the War. Meetings of the three staffs will be continued in the future whenever the need arises.

Nazi Germany is doomed. The German people will only make the cost of their defeat heavier to themselves by attempting to continue a hopeless resistance.

THE OCCUPATION AND CONTROL OF GERMANY

We have agreed on common policies and plans for enforcing the unconditional surrender terms which we shall impose together on Nazi Germany after German armed resistance has been finally crushed. These terms will not be made known until the final defeat of Germany has been accomplished. Under the agreed plan, the forces of the three powers will each occupy a separate zone of Germany. Coordinated administration and control has been provided for under the plan through a central control commission consisting of the Supreme Commanders of the three powers with headquarters in Berlin. It has been agreed that France should be invited by the three powers, if she should so desire, to take over a zone of occupation, and to participate as a fourth member of the control commission. The limits of the French zone will be agreed by the four governments concerned through their representatives on the European Advisory Commission.

It is our inflexible purpose to destroy German militarism and Nazism and to ensure that Germany will never again be able to disturb the peace of the world. We are determined to disarm and disband all German armed forces; break up for all time the German General Staff that has repeatedly contrived the resurgence of German militarism; remove or destroy all German military equipment; eliminate or control all German industry that could be used for military production; bring all war criminals to just and swift punishment and exact reparation in kind for the destruction wrought by the Germans; wipe out the Nazi Party, Nazi laws, organizations and institutions, remove all Nazi and militarist influences from public office and from the cultural and economic life of the German people; and take in harmony such other measures in Germany as may be necessary to the future peace and safety of the world. It is not our purpose to destroy the people of Germany, but only when Nazism and militarism have been extirpated will there be hope for a decent life for Germans, and a place for them in the comity of nations.

REPARATION BY GERMANY

We have considered the question of the damage caused by Germany to the allied nations in this war and recognized it as just that Germany be obliged to make compensation for this damage in kind to the greatest extent possible. A commission for the compensation of damage will be established. The commission will be instructed to consider the question of the extent and methods for compensating damage caused by Germany to the allied countries. The commission will work in Moscow.

UNITED NATIONS CONFERENCE

We are resolved upon the earliest possible establishment with our allies of a general international organization to maintain peace and security. We believe that this is essential, both to prevent aggression and to remove the political, economic and social causes of war through the close and continuing collaboration of all peace-loving peoples.

The foundations were laid at Dumbarton Oaks. On the

important question of voting procedure, however, agreement was not there reached. The present Conference has been able to resolve this difficulty.

We have agreed that a conference of United Nations should be called to meet at San Francisco in the United States on April 25, 1945, to prepare the charter of such an organization, along the lines proposed in the informal conversations at Dumbarton Oaks.

The Government of China and the Provisional Government of France will be immediately consulted and invited to sponsor invitations to the conference jointly with the Governments of the United States, Great Britain and the Union of Soviet Socialist Republics. As soon as the consultation with China and France has been completed, the text of the proposals on voting procedure will be made public.

DECLARATION ON LIBERATED EUROPE

The Premier of the Union of Soviet Socialist Republics, the Prime Minister of the United Kingdom, and the President of the United States of America have consulted with each other in the common interests of the peoples of their countries and those of liberated Europe. They jointly declare their mutual agreement to concert during the temporary period of instability in liberated Europe the policies of their three governments in assisting the peoples liberated from the domination of Nazi Germany and the peoples of the former Axis satellite states of Europe to solve by democratic means their pressing political and economic problems.

The establishment of order in Europe and the rebuilding of national economic life must be achieved by processes which will enable the liberated peoples to destroy the last vestiges of Nazism and Fascism and to create democratic institutions of their own choice. This is a principle of the Atlantic Charter—the right of all peoples to choose the form of government under which they will live—the restoration of sovereign rights and self-government to those peoples who have been forcibly deprived of them by the aggressor nations.

To foster the conditions in which the liberated peoples may exercise these rights, the three governments will jointly assist the people in any European liberated state or former Axis satellite state in Europe where in their judgment conditions require (A) to establish conditions of internal peace; (B) to carry out emergency measures for the relief of distressed peoples; (C) to form interim governmental authorities broadly representative of all democratic elements in the population and pledged to the earliest possible establishment through free elections of governments responsive to the will of the people; and (D) to facilitate where necessary the holding of such elections.

The three governments will consult the other United Nations and provisional authorities or other governments in Europe when matters of direct interest to them are under consideration.

When, in the opinion of the three governments, conditions in any European liberated state or any former Axis satellite state in Europe make such action necessary, they will immediately consult together on the measures necessary to discharge the joint responsibilities set forth in this declaration.

By this declaration we reaffirm our faith in the principles of the Atlantic Charter, our pledge in the declaration by the United Nations, and our determination to build in cooperation with other peace-loving nations world order under law, dedicated to peace, security, freedom and general well-being of all mankind.

In issuing this declaration, the three powers express the hope that the Provisional Government of the French Republic may be associated with them in the procedure suggested.

POLAND

A new situation has been created in Poland as a result of her complete liberation by the Red Army. This calls for the establishment of a Polish provisional government which can be more broadly based than was possible before the recent liberation of Western Poland. The provisional government which is now functioning in Poland should therefore be reorganized on a broader democratic basis with the inclusion of democratic leaders from Poland itself and from Poles abroad. This new government should then be called the Polish Provisional Government of National Unity.

M. Molotov, Mr. Harriman and Sir A. Clark-Kerr are authorized as a commission to consult in the first instance in Moscow with members of the present provisional government and with other Polish democratic leaders from within Poland and from abroad, with a view to the reorganization of the present government along the above lines. This Polish Provisional Government of National Unity shall be pledged to the holding of free and unfettered elections as soon as possible on the basis of universal suffrage and secret ballot. In these elections all democratic and anti-Nazi parties shall have the right to take part and to put forward candidates.

When a Polish Provisional Government of National Unity has been properly formed in conformity with the above, the government of the U.S.S.R., which now maintains diplomatic relations with the present provisional government of Poland, and the government of the United Kingdom and the government of the U.S.A. will establish diplomatic relations with the new Polish Provisional Government of National Unity, and will exchange ambassadors by whose reports the respective governments will be kept informed about the situation in Poland.

The three heads of government consider that the Eastern frontier of Poland should follow the Curzon line with digressions from it in some regions of five to eight kilometres in favour of Poland. They recognize that Poland must receive substantial accessions of territory in the North and West. They feel that the opinion of the new Polish Provisional Government of National Unity should be sought in due course on the extent of these accessions and that the final delimitation of the western frontier of Poland should thereafter await the peace conference.

YUGOSLAVIA

We have agreed to recommend to Marshal Tito and Dr. Subasitch that the agreement between them should be put into effect immediately, and that a new government should be formed on the basis of that agreement.

We also recommend that as soon as the new government has been formed it should declare that:

(1) The anti-Fascist assembly of National Liberation (Avnoj) should be extended to include members of the last Yugoslav Parliament (Skupschina) who have not compromised themselves by collaboration with the enemy, thus forming a body to be known as a temporary Parliament; and,

(2) Legislative acts passed by the anti-Fascist Assembly

of National Liberation will be subject to subsequent ratification by a constituent assembly.

There was also a general review of other Balkan questions.

MEETINGS OF FOREIGN SECRETARIES

Throughout the Conference, besides the daily meetings of the heads of governments and the Foreign Secretaries, separate meetings of the three Foreign Secretaries, and their advisers have also been held daily.

These meetings have proved of the utmost value and the Conference agreed that permanent machinery should be set up for regular consultation between the three Foreign Secretaries. They will, therefore, meet as often as may be necessary, probably about every three or four months. These meetings will be held in rotation in the three capitals, the first meeting being held in London, after the United Nations Conference on World Organization.

UNITY FOR PEACE AS FOR WAR

Our meeting here in the Crimea has reaffirmed our common determination to maintain and strengthen in the peace to come that unity of purpose and of action which has made victory possible and certain for the United Nations in this war. We believe that this is a sacred obligation which our Governments owe to our peoples and to all the peoples of the world.

Only with the continuing and growing cooperation and understanding among our three countries and among all the peace-loving nations can the highest aspiration of humanity be realized—a secure and lasting peace which will, in the words of the Atlantic Charter, "afford assurance that all the men in all the lands may live out their lives in freedom from fear and want."

Victory in this war and establishment of the proposed international organization will provide the greatest opportunity in all history to create in the years to come the essential conditions of such a peace.

Signed: WINSTON S. CHURCHILL
FRANKLIN D. ROOSEVELT
J. STALIN

February 11, 1945.

THE ACT OF CHAPULTEPEC *

DECLARATION ON RECIPROCAL ASSISTANCE AND AMERICAN SOLIDARITY

WHEREAS:

1. The peoples of the Americas, animated by a profound love of justice, remain sincerely devoted to the principles of international law:

2. It is their desire that such principles, notwithstanding the present difficult circumstances, may prevail with greater force in future international relations:

3. The Inter-American Conferences have repeatedly proclaimed certain fundamental principles, but these must be reaffirmed and proclaimed at a time when the juridical bases of the community of nations are being established:

4. The new situation in the world makes more imperative than ever the union and solidarity of the American peoples, for the defense of their rights and the maintenance of international peace:

5. The American states have been incorporating in their international law, since 1890, by means of conventions, resolutions and declarations, the following principles:

(a) The proscription of territorial conquest and the non-recognition of all acquisitions made by force (First International Conference of American States, 1890).

(b) The condemnation of intervention by a State in the

* Department of State, *Bulletin*, March 4, 1945.

internal or external affairs of another (Seventh International Conference of American States, 1933, and Inter-American Conference for the Maintenance of Peace, 1936).

(c) The recognition that every war or threat of war affects directly or indirectly all civilized peoples, and endangers the great principles of liberty and justice which constitute the American ideal and the standard of its international policy (Inter-American Conference for the Maintenance of Peace, 1936).

(d) The procedure of mutual consultation in order to find means of peaceful cooperation in the event of war or threat of war between American countries (Inter-American Conference for the Maintenance of Peace, 1936).

(e) The recognition that every act susceptible of disturbing the peace of America affects each and every one of them and justifies the initiation of the procedure of consultation (Inter-American Conference for the Maintenance of Peace, 1936).

(f) That any difference or dispute between the American nations, whatever its nature or origin, shall be settled by the methods of conciliation, or unrestricted arbitration, or through the operation of international justice (Inter-American Conference for the Maintenance of Peace, 1936).

(g) The recognition that respect for the personality, sovereignty and independence of each American State constitutes the essence of international order sustained by continental solidarity, which historically has been expressed and sustained by declarations and treaties in force (Eighth International Conference of American States, 1938).

(h) The affirmation that respect for and the faithful observance of treaties constitutes the indispensable rule for the development of peaceful relations between States, and treaties can only be revised by agreement of the contracting parties (Declaration of American Principles, Eighth International Conference of American States, 1938).

(i) That in case the peace, security or territorial integrity of any American republic is threatened by acts of any nature that may impair them, they proclaim their common concern and their determination to make effective their solidarity, coordinating their respective sovereign wills by means of the procedure of consultation, using the measures which in each case the circumstances may make advisable (Declaration of Lima, Eighth International Conference of American States, 1938).

(j) That any attempt on the part of a non-American State against the integrity or inviolability of the territory, the sovereignty or the political independence of an American State shall be considered as an act of aggression against all the American States (Declaration XV of the Second Meeting of the Ministers of Foreign Affairs, Habana, 1940).

6. The furtherance of these principles, which the American States have practiced in order to secure peace and solidarity between the nations of the Continent constitutes an effective means of contributing to the general system of world security and of facilitating its establishment: and

7. The security and solidarity of the Continent are affected to the same extent by an act of aggression against any of the American States by a non-American State, as by an American State against one or more American states.

PART I

Declaration

THE GOVERNMENTS REPRESENTED AT THE INTER-AMERI-
CAN CONFERENCE ON WAR AND PEACE

DECLARE:

First. That all sovereign States are juridically equal amongst themselves.

Second. That every state has the right to the respect of its individuality and independence, on the part of the other members of the international community.

Third. That every attack of a State against the integrity or the inviolability of territory, or against the sovereignty or political independence of an American State, shall, conformably to Part III hereof, be considered as an act of aggression against the other States which sign this declaration. In any case invasion by armed forces of one State into the territory of another, trespassing boundaries established by treaty and demarcated in accordance therewith shall constitute an act of aggression.

Fourth. That in case acts of aggression occur or there may be reasons to believe that an aggression is being prepared by any other State against the integrity and inviolability of territory, or against the sovereignty or political independence of an American State, the States signatory to this declaration will consult amongst themselves in order to agree upon measures it may be advisable to take.

Fifth. That during the war, and until the treaty recommended in Part II hereof is concluded, the signatories of this declaration recognize that such threats and acts of aggression as indicated in paragraphs Third and Fourth above constitute an interference with the war effort of the United Nations, calling for such procedures, within the scope of their constitutional powers of a general nature and for war, as may be found necessary, including:

recall of chiefs of diplomatic missions;

breaking of diplomatic relations;

breaking of consular relations;

breaking of postal, telegraphic, telephonic, radio-telephonic relations;

interruption of economic, commercial and financial relations;

use of armed force to prevent or repel aggression.

Sixth. That the principles and procedure contained in this declaration shall become effective immediately, inasmuch as any act of aggression or threat of aggression during the present state of war interferes with the war effort of the United Nations to obtain victory. Henceforth, and with the view that the principles and procedure herein stipulated shall conform with the constitutional principles of each republic, the respective Governments shall take the necessary steps to perfect this instrument in order that it shall be in force at all times.

PART II

Recommendation

THE INTER-AMERICAN CONFERENCE ON PROBLEMS OF WAR AND PEACE

RECOMMENDS:

That for the purpose of meeting threats or acts of aggression against any American Republic following the establishment of peace, the Governments of the American Republics should consider the conclusion, in accordance with their constitutional processes, of a treaty establishing procedures whereby such threats or acts may be met by:

The use, by all or some of the signatories of said treaty of any one or more of the following measures:

recall of chiefs of diplomatic missions;

breaking of diplomatic relations;

breaking of consular relations;

breaking of postal, telegraphic, telephonic, radio-telephonic relations;

interruption of economic, commercial and financial relations;

use of armed force to prevent or repel aggression.

PART III

This declaration and recommendation provide for a regional arrangement for dealing with matters relating to the maintenance of international peace and security as are appropriate for regional action in this Hemisphere and said arrangements and the activities and procedures referred to therein shall be consistent with the purposes and principles of the general international organization, when established.

This declaration and recommendation shall be known as the *ACT OF CHAPULTEPEC*.

TREATY BETWEEN THE SOVIET UNION AND THE UNITED KINGDOM

May 26, 1942 *

DESIRING to confirm the stipulations of the agreement between His Majesty's Government in the United Kingdom and the Government of the U.S.S.R. for joint action in the war against Germany signed at Moscow July 12, 1941, and to replace them by a formal treaty;

Desiring to contribute after the war to the maintenance of peace and to prevent further aggression by Germany or the States associated with her in her acts of aggression in Europe;

Desiring, moreover, to give expression to their intention of collaborating closely with one another as well as with the United Nations at the peace settlement and during the ensuing period of reconstruction on the basis of the principles enunciated in the declaration made on August 14, 1941, by the President of the United States of America and the Prime Minister of the United Kingdom of Great Britain and Northern Ireland to which the Government of the Union of Socialist Soviet Republics has adhered;

Desiring finally to provide for mutual assistance in the event of an attack upon either of the high contracting parties by Germany or any of the States associated with her in acts of aggression in Europe.

* *The United States News*, "The United States and the Peace," Part I, A Collection of Documents, August 14, 1941, to March 5, 1945.

PART ONE

Article 1. In virtue of the alliance established between the United Kingdom and the U.S.S.R., the high contracting parties mutually undertake to afford one another military and other assistance and support of all kinds in the war against Germany and all those States which are associated with her in acts of aggression in Europe.

Article 2. The high contracting parties undertake not to enter into any negotiations with Hitlerite Government or any other Government in Germany that does not clearly renounce all aggressive intentions and not to negotiate or conclude except by mutual consent any armistice or peace treaty with Germany or any other State associated with her in acts of aggression in Europe.

PART TWO

Article 3. (1) The high contracting parties declare their desire to unite with other like-minded States in adopting proposals for common action to preserve peace and resist aggression in the post-war period.

(2) Pending the adoption of such proposals they will after the termination of hostilities take all measures in their power to render impossible a repetition of aggression and violation of peace by Germany or any of the States associated with her in acts of aggression in Europe.

Article 4. Should one of the high contracting parties during the post-war period become involved in hostilities with Germany or any of the States mentioned in Article 3 (2) in consequence of an attack by that State against that party, the other high contracting party will at once give to the contracting party so involved in hostilities all military and other support and assistance in her power.

This Article shall remain in force until the high contracting parties by mutual agreement shall recognize that it is superseded by the adoption of the proposals contemplated in Article 3 (1). In default of the adoption of such proposals it shall remain in force for a period of 20 years and thereafter until terminated by either high contracting party as provided in Article 8.

Article 5. The high contracting parties having regard to the interests of the security of each of them agree to work together in close and friendly collaboration after the re-establishment of peace for the organization of security and economic prosperity in Europe. They will take into account the interests of the United Nations in these objects and they will act in accordance with the two principles of not seeking territorial aggrandisement for themselves and of non-interference in the internal affairs of other States.

Article 6. The high contracting parties agree to render one another all possible economic assistance after the war.

Article 7. Each high contracting party undertakes not to conclude any alliance and not to take part in any coalition directed against the other high contracting party.

Article 8. The present treating is subject to ratification in the shortest possible time and instruments of ratification shall be exchanged in Moscow as soon as possible.

It comes into force immediately on the exchange of instruments of ratification and shall thereupon replace the agreement between the Government of the U.S.S.R. and His Majesty's Government in the United Kingdom at Moscow on July 12, 1941.

Part 1 of the present treaty shall remain in force until

the re-establishment of peace between the high contracting parties and Germany and the powers associated with her in acts of aggression in Europe.

Part 2 of the present treaty shall remain in force for a period of 20 years. Thereafter unless 12 months' notice has been given by either party to terminate the treaty at the end of the said period of 20 years it shall continue in force until 12 months after either high contracting party shall have given notice to the other in writing of his intention to terminate it.

FRANCO-SOVIET ALLIANCE *

THE Provisional Government of the French Republic and the Presidium of the Supreme Council of the Union of Socialist Soviet Republics.

Determined to prosecute jointly, and to the end, the war against Germany;

Convinced that once victory is achieved, the re-establishment of peace on a stable basis and its prolonged maintenance in the future will be conditioned by the existence of close collaboration between them and with all the United Nations;

Having resolved to collaborate in the cause of the creation of an international system of security for the effective maintenance of general peace and for ensuring harmonious development of relations between nations;

Desirous of confirming mutual obligations resulting from the exchange of letters of September 26, 1941, concerning joint actions in the war against Germany;

Convinced that the conclusion of an alliance between the U.S.S.R. and France corresponds to the sentiments and interests of both peoples, the demands of the war and the requirements of peace and economic reconstruction in full conformity with the aims which the United Nations set themselves;

* *The United Nations Review*, January 15, 1945, p. 9.

Decided to conclude a Treaty to this effect and appointed as their Plenipotentiaries:

The Provisional Government of the French Republic— Georges Bidault, Minister of Foreign Affairs; who, after the exchange of their credentials, found in due form and good order, agreed on the following: The Presidium of the Supreme Soviet of the Union of Soviet Socialist Republics— Vyacheslav Mikhailovich Molotov, People's Commissar for Foreign Affairs of the U.S.S.R.;

ARTICLE I: Each of the High Contracting Parties shall continue the struggle on the side of the other Party and on the side of the United Nations until final victory over Germany. Each of the High Contracting Parties undertakes to render the other Party aid and assistance in this struggle with all the means at its disposal.

ARTICLE II: The High Contracting Parties shall not agree to enter into separate negotiations with Germany or to conclude without mutual consent any Armistice or Peace Treaty either with the Hitler Government or with any other Government or authority set up in Germany for the purpose of the continuation or support of the policy of German aggression.

ARTICLE III: The High Contracting Parties undertake also after the termination of the present war with Germany to take jointly all necessary measures for the elimination of any new threat coming from Germany and to obstruct such actions as would make possible any new attempt at aggression on her part.

ARTICLE IV: In the event of either of the High Contracting Parties finding itself involved in military operations against Germany whether as a result of aggression committed by the latter or as a result of the operation of the above Article III, the other Party shall at once render it every aid and assistance within its power.

ARTICLE V: The High Contracting Parties undertake not to conclude any Alliance and not to take part in any coalition directed against either of the High Contracting Parties.

ARTICLE VI: The High Contracting Parties agree to render each other every possible economic assistance after the war with a view to facilitating and accelerating the reconstruction of both countries and in order to contribute to the cause of world prosperity.

ARTICLE VII: The present Treaty does not in any way affect obligations undertaken previously by the High Contracting Parties in regard to third states in virtue of published Treaties.

ARTICLE VIII: The present Treaty, the Russian and French texts of which are equally valid, shall be ratified and ratification instruments shall be exchanged in Paris as early as possible. It comes into force from the moment of the exchange of ratification instruments and shall be valid for twenty years. If the Treaty is not denounced by either of the High Contracting Parties at least one year before the expiration of this term, it shall remain valid for an unlimited time, each of the Contracting Parties being able to terminate its operation by giving notice to that effect one year in advance.

In confirmation of which the above Plenipotentiaries signed the present Treaty and affixed their seals thereto.

Done in Moscow in two copies. December 10, 1944.

BIDAULT	MOLOTOV
Minister of	Commissar for
Foreign Affairs	Foreign Affairs

RUSSIAN-CZECHOSLOVAK MUTUAL ASSISTANCE TREATY *

The President of the Supreme Soviet of the U.S.S.R. and the President of the Czechoslovak Republic.

In their desire to confirm the terms of the agreement between the U.S.S.R. and the Government of the Czechoslovak Republic signed at Prague May 16, 1935, and

In their desire to confirm the terms of the agreement between the U.S.S.R. and the Government of the Czechoslovak Republic about joint action in the war against Germany, signed at London, July 18, 1941,

In their desire to contribute after the war to the maintenance of peace and the prevention of further aggression on the part of Germany, and

To assure permanent friendship and postwar peaceful collaboration amongst themselves,

Have decided to conclude for this purpose an agreement and have appointed with this purpose as their plenipotentiaries:

The Presidium of the Supreme Soviet of the U.S.S.R.: V. M. Molotov, People's Commissar for Foreign Affairs:

The President of the Czechoslovak Republic: Zdenek Fierlinger, Ambassador of the Czechoslovak Republic:

Who, having exchanged their credentials, which have

* *The United Nations Review*, January 15, 1944, p. 14. The text of the Russian-Czechoslovak Mutual Assistance Treaty, as broadcast by the Moscow radio and recorded by the United Press.

been found in perfect order, have drawn up in appropriate form and have agreed as follows:

ARTICLE I

The high contracting powers agree to unite in a policy of permanent friendship and friendly postwar collaboration, as well as mutual assistance of all kinds in the present war against Germany and all such states as are bound with her in acts of aggression in Europe.

ARTICLE II

The two high contracting powers undertake for the period of the war not to enter any sort of negotiations with the Hitlerite Government or any other Government of Germany which does not explicitly renounce all aggressive intentions, and also not to engage in negotiations toward or to conclude without mutual agreement any sort of treaty of peace with Germany or any other state bound with her in acts of aggression in Europe.

ARTICLE III

Reaffirming their pre-war policy of peace and mutual assistance, as expressed in the agreement signed at Prague on May 16, 1935, the high contracting powers undertake that in case one of them finds herself, in the postwar period, involved in hostilities with Germany, renewing her policy of *Drang nach Osten,* or with any other state that may unite with Germany directly or in any other form in such a war, then the other high contracting power will immediately render to the other contracting power thus involved in hostilities every military and other support and assistance within its power.

ARTICLE IV

The high contracting powers in the interest of each other's security agree to close and friendly collaboration in the period after the conclusion of peace and to act in accordance with the principles of mutual respect of their independence and sovereignty as well as non-interference in the internal affairs of the other State.

They agree to carry out economic relations between each other on the largest possible scale and to render each other all possible economic assistance after the war.

ARTICLE V

Each of the high contracting powers undertakes not to conclude any alliance and not to take part in any coalition directed against the other contracting power.

ARTICLE VI

The present agreement comes into force immediately after its signature and is subject to ratification at the earliest possible date. The exchange of ratification documents will take place at Moscow as early as possible. The present agreement remains in force for twenty years after signature, whereby if one of the high contracting powers will not make a declaration twelve months before its expiration to the effect that it desires to renounce the agreement this agreement will continue to remain in force for a further period of five years. And so every time until one of the high contracting powers gives notice twelve months before the expiration of the current five-year period. In testimony whereof the plenipotentiaries have signed the present agreement and have put their stamps on it. The agreements have

been drawn up in the Russian and Czechoslovak languages.
Both texts have equal force.

Moscow, 12 December 1943

The plenipotentiary of the Presidium
of the Supreme Soviet of the U.S.S.R. MOLOTOV.

The plenipotentiary of the President of the
Czechoslovak Republic FIERLINGER.

*Protocol to the Agreement of Mutual Friendship, Mutual
Assistance and Postwar Collaboration between the
U.S.S.R. and the Czechoslovak Republic, Concluded
12 December, 1943.*

The high contracting powers are agreed with regard to
the conclusion of this present agreement of friendship, mutual assistance and postwar collaboration between the
U.S.S.R. and the Czechoslovak Republic that should any
third power bordering on the U.S.S.R. or the Czechoslovak
Republic, and representing in this war an object of German
aggression, express a desire to join the present agreement,
the latter will be given the possibility of signing this agreement on the mutual agreement of the U.S.S.R. and the
Czechoslovak Republic, thus making it a tripartite agreement.

The present protocol is drawn up in two copies in the
Russian and Czechoslovak language, each text having equal
force.

Moscow, 12 December 1943

Plenipotentiary of the Presidium of the
Supreme Soviet of the U.S.S.R. MOLOTOV.

Plenipotentiary of the President of the
Czechoslovak Republic FIERLINGER.

CHARTER OF THE UNITED NATIONS *

WE THE PEOPLES OF THE UNITED NATIONS DETERMINED

—to save succeeding generations from the scourge of war, which twice in our lifetime has brought untold sorrow to mankind, and

—to reaffirm faith in fundamental human rights, in the dignity and worth of the human person, in the equal rights of men and women and of nations large and small, and

—to establish conditions under which justice and respect for the obligations arising from treaties and other sources of international law can be maintained, and

—to promote social progress and better standards of life in larger freedom,

AND FOR THESE ENDS

—to practice tolerance and live together in peace with one another as good neighbors, and

—to unite our strength to maintain international peace and security, and

—to ensure, by the acceptance of principles and the institution of methods, that armed force shall not be used, save in the common interest, and

—to employ international machinery for the promotion of the economic and social advancement of all peoples,

* *Charter of the United Nations, Report to the President on the Results of the San Francisco Conference by the Chairman of the United States Delegation, the Secretary of State.* Department of State, Publication 2349, Conference Series 71, June 26, 1945.

HAVE RESOLVED TO COMBINE OUR EFFORTS TO ACCOMPLISH THESE AIMS.

Accordingly, our respective governments, through representatives assembled in the city of San Francisco, who have exhibited their full powers found to be in good and due form, have agreed to the present Charter of the United Nations and do hereby establish an international organization to be known as the United Nations.

CHAPTER I

PURPOSES AND PRINCIPLES

Article 1

The purposes of the United Nations are:

1. To maintain international peace and security, and to that end: to take effective collective measures for the prevention and removal of threats to the peace, and for the suppression of acts of aggression or other breaches of the peace, and to bring about by peaceful means, and in conformity with the principles of justice and international law, adjustment or settlement of international disputes or situations which might lead to a breach of the peace;

2. To develop friendly relations among nations based on respect for the principle of equal rights and self-determination of peoples, and to take other appropriate measures to strengthen universal peace;

3. To achieve international cooperation in solving international problems of an economic, social, cultural, or humanitarian character, and in promoting and encouraging respect for human rights and for fundamental freedoms for all without distinction as to race, sex, language, or religion; and

4. To be a center for harmonizing the actions of nations in the attainment of these common ends.

Article 2

The organization and its members, in pursuit of the purposes stated in Article 1, shall act in accordance with the following principles:

1. The organization is based on the principle of the sovereign equality of all its members.

2. All members, in order to ensure to all of them the rights and benefits resulting from membership, shall fulfill in good faith the obligations assumed by them in accordance with the present Charter.

3. All members shall settle their international disputes by peaceful means in such a manner that international peace and security, and justice, are not endangered.

4. All members shall refrain in their international relations from the threat or use of force against the territorial integrity or political independence of any state, or in any other manner inconsistent with the purposes of the United Nations.

5. All members shall give the United Nations every assistance in any action it takes in accordance with the present Charter, and shall refrain from giving assistance to any state against which the United Nations is taking preventive or enforcement action.

6. The organization shall ensure that states which are not members of the United Nations act in accordance with these principles so far as may be necessary for the maintenance of international peace and security.

7. Nothing contained in the present Charter shall authorize the United Nations to intervene in matters which are

essentially within the domestic jurisdiction of any state or shall require the members to submit such matters to settlement under the present Charter; but this principle shall not prejudice the application of enforcement measures under Chapter VII.

CHAPTER II

MEMBERSHIP

Article 3

The original members of the United Nations shall be the states which, having participated in the United Nations Conference on International Organization at San Francisco or having previously signed the Declaration by United Nations of January 1, 1942, sign the present Charter and ratify it in accordance with Article 110.

Article 4

1. Membership in the United Nations is open to all other peace-loving states which accept the obligations contained in the present Charter and, in the judgment of the organization, are able and willing to carry out these obligations.

2. The admission of any such state to membership in the United Nations will be effected by a decision of the General Assembly upon the recommendation of the Security Council.

Article 5

A member of the United Nations against which preventive or enforcement action has been taken by the Security Council may be suspended from the exercise of the rights and privileges of membership by the General Assembly upon the recommendation of the Security Council. The exercise of these rights and privileges may be restored by the Security Council.

Article 6

A member of the United Nations which has persistently violated the principles contained in the present Charter may be expelled from the organization by the General Assembly upon the recommendation of the Security Council.

CHAPTER III

ORGANS

Article 7

1. There are established as the principal organs of the United Nations: a General Assembly, a Security Council, an Economic and Social Council, a Trusteeship Council, an International Court of Justice, and a Secretariat.

2. Such subsidiary organs as may be found necessary may be established in accordance with the present Charter.

Article 8

The United Nations shall place no restrictions on the eligibility of men and women to participate in any capacity and under conditions of equality in its principal and subsidiary organs.

CHAPTER IV

THE GENERAL ASSEMBLY

COMPOSITION

Article 9

1. The General Assembly shall consist of all the members of the United Nations.

2. Each member shall have not more than five representatives in the General Assembly.

Functions and Powers

Article 10

The General Assembly may discuss any questions or any matters within the scope of the present Charter or relating to the powers and functions of any organs provided in the present Charter, and, except as provided for in Article 12, may make recommendations to the members of the United Nations or to the Security Council or to both on any such questions or matters.

Article 11

1. The General Assembly may consider the general principles of cooperation in the maintenance of international peace and security, including the principles governing disarmament and the regulation of armaments, and may make recommendations with regard to such principles to the members or to the Security Council or to both.

2. The General Assembly may discuss any questions relating to the maintenance of international peace and security brought before it by any member of the United Nations, or by the Security Council, or by a state which is not a member of the United Nations in accordance with Article 35, paragraph 2, and, except as provided in Article 12, may make recommendations with regard to any such questions to the state or states concerned or to the Security Council or to both. Any such question on which action is necessary shall be referred to the Security Council by the General Assembly either before or after discussion.

3. The General Assembly may call the attention of the Security Council to situations which are likely to endanger international peace and security.

4. The powers of the General Assembly set forth in this article shall not limit the general scope of Article 10.

Article 12

1. While the Security Council is exercising in respect of any dispute or situation the functions assigned to it in the present Charter, the General Assembly shall not make any recommendation with regard to that dispute or situation unless the Security Council so requests.

2. The Secretary-General, with the consent of the Security Council, shall notify the General Assembly at each session of any matters relative to the maintenance of international peace and security which are being dealt with by the Security Council and shall similarly notify the General Assembly, or the members of the United Nations if the General Assembly is not in session, immediately the Security Council ceases to deal with such matters.

Article 13

1. The General Assembly shall initiate studies and make recommendations for the purpose of:

a. Promoting international cooperation in the political field and encouraging the progressive development of international law and its codification;

b. Promoting international cooperation in the economic, social, cultural, educational, and health fields, and assisting in the realization of human rights and fundamental freedoms for all without distinction as to race, sex, language, or religion.

2. The further responsibilities, functions, and powers of the General Assembly with respect to matters mentioned in paragraph 1 (b) above are set forth in Chapters IX and X.

Article 14

Subject to the provisions of Article 12, the General Assembly may recommend measures for the peaceful adjustment of any situation, regardless of origin, which it deems likely to impair the general welfare or friendly relations among nations, including situations resulting from a violation of the provisions of the present Charter setting forth the purposes and principles of the United Nations.

Article 15

1. The General Assembly shall receive and consider annual and special reports from the Security Council; these reports shall include an account of the measures that the Security Council has decided upon or taken to maintain international peace and security.

2. The General Assembly shall receive and consider reports from the other organs of the United Nations.

Article 16

The General Assembly shall perform such functions with respect to the international trusteeship system as are assigned to it under Chapters XII and XIII, including the approval of the trusteeship agreements for areas not designated as strategic.

Article 17

1. The General Assembly shall consider and approve the budget of the organization.

2. The expenses of the organization shall be borne by the members as apportioned by the General Assembly.

3. The General Assembly shall consider and approve any financial and budgetary arrangements with specialized agencies referred to in Article 57 and shall examine the administrative budgets of such specialized agencies with a view to making recommendations to the agencies concerned.

VOTING

Article 18

1. Each member of the General Assembly shall have one vote.

2. Decisions of the General Assembly on important questions shall be made by a two-thirds majority of the members present and voting. These questions shall include: recommendations with respect to the maintenance of international peace and security, the election of the non-permanent members of the Security Council, the election of the members of the Economic and Social Council, the election of the members of the Trusteeship Council in accordance with paragraph 1 (c) of Article 86, the admission of new members to the United Nations, the suspension of the rights and privileges of membership, the expulsion of members, questions relating to the operation of the trusteeship system, and budgetary questions.

3. Decisions on other questions, including the determination of additional categories of questions to be decided by a two-thirds majority, shall be made by a majority of the members present and voting.

Article 19

A member of the United Nations which is in arrears in the payment of its financial contributions to the organization shall have no vote in the General Assembly if the amount of its arrears equals or exceeds the amount of the contributions due from it for the preceding two full years. The General Assembly may, nevertheless, permit such a member to vote if it is satisfied that the failure to pay is due to conditions beyond the control of the member.

PROCEDURE

Article 20

The General Assembly shall meet in regular annual sessions and in such special sessions as occasion may require. Special sessions shall be convoked by the Secretary-General at the request of the Security Council or of a majority of the members of the United Nations.

Article 21

The General Assembly shall adopt its own rules of procedure. It shall elect its President for each session.

Article 22

The General Assembly may establish such subsidiary organs as it deems necessary for the performance of its functions.

CHAPTER V

THE SECURITY COUNCIL

COMPOSITION

Article 23

1. The Security Council shall consist of eleven members of the United Nations. The Republic of China, France, the Union of Soviet Socialist Republics, the United Kingdom of Great Britain and Northern Ireland, and the United States of America shall be permanent members of the Security Council. The General Assembly shall elect six other members of the United Nations to be non-permanent members of the Security Council, due regard being specially paid, in the first instance to the contribution of members of the United Nations to the maintenance of international peace and security and to the other purposes of the organization, and also to equitable geographical distribution.

2. The non-permanent members of the Security Council shall be elected for a term of two years. In the first election of the non-permanent members, however, three shall be chosen for a term of one year. A retiring member shall not be eligible for immediate re-election.

3. Each member of the Security Council shall have one representative.

FUNCTIONS AND POWERS

Article 24

1. In order to ensure prompt and effective action by the United Nations, its members confer on the Security Council primary responsibility for the maintenance of international

peace and security, and agree that in carrying out its duties under this responsibility the Security Council acts on their behalf.

2. In discharging these duties the Security Council shall act in accordance with the purposes and principles of the United Nations. The specific powers granted to the Security Council for the discharge of these duties are laid down in Chapters VI, VII, VIII, and XII.

3. The Security Council shall submit annual and, when necessary, special reports to the General Assembly for its consideration.

Article 25

The members of the United Nations agree to accept and carry out the decisions of the Security Council in accordance with the present Charter.

Article 26

In order to promote the establishment and maintenance of international peace and security with the least diversion for armaments of the world's human and economic resources, the Security Council shall be responsible for formulating, with the assistance of the Military Staff Committee referred to in Article 47, plans to be submitted to the members of the United Nations for the establishment of a system for the regulation of armaments.

VOTING

Article 27

1. Each member of the Security Council shall have one vote.

2. Decisions of the Security Council on procedural matters shall be made by an affirmative vote of seven members.

3. Decisions of the Security Council on all other matters shall be made by an affirmative vote of seven members including the concurring votes of the permanent members; provided that, in decisions under Chapter VI, and under paragraph 3 of Article 52, a party to a dispute shall abstain from voting.

PROCEDURE

Article 28

1. The Security Council shall be so organized as to be able to function continuously. Each member of the Security Council shall for this purpose be represented at all times at the seat of the organization.

2. The Security Council shall hold periodic meetings at which each of its members may, if it so desires, be represented by a member of the government or by some other specially designated representative.

3. The Security Council may hold meetings at such places other than the seat of the organization as in its judgment will best facilitate its work.

Article 29

The Security Council may establish such subsidiary organs as it deems necessary for the performance of its functions.

Article 30

The Security Council shall adopt its own rules of procedure, including the method of selecting its President.

Article 31

Any member of the United Nations which is not a member of the Security Council may participate, without vote, in the discussion of any question brought before the Security Council whenever the latter considers that the interests of that member are specially affected.

Article 32

Any member of the United Nations which is not a member of the Security Council or any state which is not a member of the United Nations, if it is a party to a dispute under consideration by the Security Council, shall be invited to participate, without vote, in the discussion relating to the dispute. The Security Council shall lay down such conditions as it deems just for the participation of a state which is not a member of the United Nations.

CHAPTER VI

PACIFIC SETTLEMENT OF DISPUTES

Article 33

1. The parties to any dispute, the continuance of which is likely to endanger the maintenance of international peace and security, shall, first of all, seek a solution by negotiation, enquiry, mediation, conciliation, arbitration, judicial settlement, resort to regional agencies or arrangements, or other peaceful means of their own choice.

2. The Security Council shall, when it deems necessary, call upon the parties to settle their dispute by such means.

Article 34

The Security Council may investigate any dispute, or any situation which might lead to international friction or give rise to a dispute, in order to determine whether the continuance of the dispute or situation is likely to endanger the maintenance of international peace and security.

Article 35

1. Any member of the United Nations may bring any dispute or any situation of the nature referred to in Article 34 to the attention of the Security Council or of the General Assembly.

2. A state which is not a member of the United Nations may bring to the attention of the Security Council or of the General Assembly any dispute to which it is a party if it accepts in advance, for the purposes of the dispute, the obligations of pacific settlement provided in the present Charter.

3. The proceedings of the General Assembly in respect of matters brought to its attention under this article will be subject to the provisions of Articles 11 and 12.

Article 36

1. The Security Council may, at any stage of a dispute of the nature referred to in Article 33 or of a situation of like nature, recommend appropriate procedures or methods of adjustment.

2. The Security Council should take into consideration any procedures for the settlement of the dispute which have already been adopted by the parties.

3. In making recommendations under this article the Security Council should also take into consideration that legal

disputes should as a general rule be referred by the parties to the International Court of Justice in accordance with the provisions of the Statute of the Court.

Article 37

1. Should the parties to a dispute of the nature referred to in Article 33 fail to settle it by the means indicated in that article, they shall refer it to the Security Council.

2. If the Security Council deems that the continuance of the dispute is in fact likely to endanger the maintenance of international peace and security, it shall decide whether to take action under Article 36 or to recommend such terms of settlement as it may consider appropriate.

Article 38

Without prejudice to the provisions of Articles 33-37 the Security Council may, if all the parties to any dispute so request, make recommendations to the parties with a view to a pacific settlement of the dispute.

CHAPTER VII

ACTION WITH RESPECT TO THREATS TO THE PEACE, BREACHES OF THE PEACE, AND ACTS OF AGGRESSION

Article 39

The Security Council shall determine the existence of any threat to the peace, breach of the peace, or act of aggression and shall make recommendations, or decide what measures shall be taken in accordance with Articles 41 and 42, to maintain or restore international peace and security.

Article 40

In order to prevent an aggravation of the situation, the Security Council may, before making the recommendations or deciding upon the measures provided for in Article 39, call upon the parties concerned to comply with such provisional measures as it deems necessary or desirable. Such provisional measures shall be without prejudice to the rights, claims, or position of the parties concerned. The Security Council shall duly take account of failure to comply with such provisional measures.

Article 41

The Security Council may decide what measures not involving the use of armed force are to be employed to give effect to its decisions, and it may call upon the members of the United Nations to apply such measures. These may include complete or partial interruption of economic relations and of rail, sea, air, postal, telegraphic, radio, and other means of communications, and the severance of diplomatic relations.

Article 42

Should the Security Council consider that measures provided for in Article 41 would be inadequate or have proved to be inadequate, it may take such action by air, sea, or land forces as may be necessary to maintain or restore international peace and security. Such action may include demonstrations, blockade, and other operations by air, sea, or land forces of members of the United Nations.

Article 43

1. All members of the United Nations, in order to contribute to the maintenance of international peace and secu-

rity, undertake to make available to the Security Council, on its call and in accordance with a special agreement or agreements, armed forces, assistance, and facilities, including rights of passage, necessary for the purpose of maintaining international peace and security.

2. Such agreement or agreements shall govern the numbers and types of forces, their degree of readiness and general location, and the nature of the facilities and assistance to be provided.

3. The agreement or agreements shall be negotiated as soon as possible on the initiative of the Security Council. They shall be concluded between the Security Council and members or between the Security Council and groups of members and shall be subject to ratification by the signatory states in accordance with their respective constitutional processes.

Article 44

When the Security Council has decided to use force it shall, before calling upon a member not represented on it to provide armed forces in fulfilment of the obligations assumed under Article 43, invite that member, if the member so desires, to participate in the decisions of the Security Council concerning the employment of contingents of that member's armed forces.

Article 45

In order to enable the United Nations to take urgent military measures, members shall hold immediately available national air-force contingents for combined international enforcement action. The strength and degree of readiness of these contingents and plans for their combined action shall be determined, within the limits laid down in the special agreement or agreements referred to in Article 43, by the Security Council with the assistance of the Military Staff Committee.

Article 46

Plans for the application of armed force shall be made by the Security Council with the assistance of the Military Staff Committee.

Article 47

1. There shall be established a Military Staff Committee to advise and assist the Security Council on all questions relating to the Security Council's military requirements for the maintenance of international peace and security, the employment and command of forces placed at its disposal, the regulation of armaments, and possible disarmament.

2. The Military Staff Committee shall consist of the Chiefs of Staff of the permanent members of the Security Council or their representatives. Any member of the United Nations not permanently represented on the Committee shall be invited by the Committee to be associated with it when the efficient discharge of the Committee's responsibilities requires the participation of that member in its work.

3. The Military Staff Committee shall be responsible under the Security Council for the strategic direction of any armed forces placed at the disposal of the Security Council. Questions relating to the command of such forces shall be worked out subsequently.

4. The Military Staff Committee, with the authorization of the Security Council and after consultation with appropriate regional agencies, may establish regional subcommittees.

Article 48

1. The action required to carry out the decisions of the Security Council for the maintenance of international peace and security shall be taken by all the members of the United Nations or by some of them, as the Security Council may determine.

2. Such decisions shall be carried out by the members of the United Nations directly and through their action in the appropriate international agencies of which they are members.

Article 49

The members of the United Nations shall join in affording mutual assistance in carrying out the measures decided upon by the Security Council.

Article 50

If preventive or enforcement measures against any state are taken by the Security Council, any other state whether a member of the United Nations or not, which finds itself confronted with special economic problems arising from the carrying out of those measures shall have the right to consult the Security Council with regard to a solution of those problems.

Article 51

Nothing in the present Charter shall impair the inherent right of individual or collective self-defense if an armed attack occurs against a member of the United Nations, until the Security Council has taken the measures necessary to maintain international peace and security. Measures taken by members in the exercise of this right of self-defense shall be immediately reported to the Security Council and shall not in any way affect the authority and responsibility of the Security Council under the present Charter to take at any time such action as it deems necessary in order to maintain or restore international peace and security.

CHAPTER VIII

REGIONAL ARRANGEMENTS

Article 52

1. Nothing in the present Charter precludes the existence of regional arrangements or agencies for dealing with such matters relating to the maintenance of international peace and security as are appropriate for regional action, provided that such arrangements or agencies and their activities are consistent with the purposes and principles of the United Nations.

2. The members of the United Nations entering into such arrangements or constituting such agencies shall make every effort to achieve pacific settlement of local disputes through such regional arrangements or by such regional agencies before referring them to the Security Council.

3. The Security Council shall encourage the development of pacific settlement of local disputes through such regional arrangements or by such regional agencies either on the initiative of the states concerned or by reference from the Security Council.

4. This article in no way impairs the application of Articles 34 and 35.

Article 53

1. The Security Council shall, where appropriate, utilize such regional arrangements or agencies for enforcement action under its authority. But no enforcement action shall be

taken under regional arrangements or by regional agencies without the authorization of the Security Council, with the exception of measures against any enemy state, as defined in paragraph 2 of this article, provided for pursuant to Article 107 or in regional arrangements directed against renewal of aggressive policy on the part of any such state, until such time as the organization may, on request of the governments concerned, be charged with the responsibility for preventing further aggression by such a state.

2. The term enemy state as used in paragraph 1 of this article applies to any state which during the Second World War has been an enemy of any signatory of the present charter.

Article 54

The Security Council shall at all times be kept fully informed of activities undertaken or in contemplation under regional arrangements or by regional agencies for the maintenance of international peace and security.

CHAPTER IX

INTERNATIONAL ECONOMIC AND SOCIAL COOPERATION

Article 55

With a view to the creation of conditions of stability and well-being which are necessary for peaceful and friendly relations among nations based on respect for the principle of equal rights and self-determination of peoples, the United Nations shall promote:

a. Higher standards of living, full employment, and conditions of economic and social progress and development;

b. Solutions of international economic, social, health, and related problems; and international cultural and educational cooperation; and

c. Universal respect for, and observance of, human rights and fundamental freedoms for all without distinction as to race, sex, language, or religion.

Article 56

All members pledge themselves to take joint and separate action in cooperation with the organization for the achievement of the purposes set forth in Article 55.

Article 57

1. The various specialized agencies, established by intergovernmental agreement and having wide international responsibilities, as defined in their basic instruments, in economic, social, cultural, educational, health, and related fields, shall be brought into relationship with the United Nations in accordance with the provisions of Article 63.

2. Such agencies thus brought into relationship with the United Nations are hereinafter referred to as specialized agencies.

Article 58

The organization shall make recommendations for the coordination of the policies and activities of the specialized agencies.

Article 59

The organization shall, where appropriate, initiate negotiations among the states concerned for the creation of any new specialized agencies required for the accomplishment of the purposes set forth in Article 55.

Article 60

Responsibility for the discharge of the functions of the organization set forth in this chapter shall be vested in the General Assembly and, under the authority of the General Assembly, in the Economic and Social Council, which shall have for this purpose the powers set forth in Chapter X.

CHAPTER X

THE ECONOMIC AND SOCIAL COUNCIL

COMPOSITION

Article 61

1. The Economic and Social Council shall consist of eighteen members of the United Nations elected by the General Assembly.

2. Subject to the provisions of paragraph 3, six members of the Economic and Social Council shall be elected each year for a term of three years. A retiring member shall be eligible for immediate re-election.

3. At the first election, eighteen members of the Economic and Social Council shall be chosen. The term of office of six members so chosen shall expire at the end of one year, and of six other members at the end of two years, in accordance with arrangements made by the General Assembly.

4. Each member of the Economic and Social Council shall have one representative.

FUNCTIONS AND POWERS

Article 62

1. The Economic and Social Council may make or initiate studies and reports with respect to international economic, social, cultural, educational, health, and related matters and may make recommendations with respect to any such matters to the General Assembly, to the members of the United Nations, and to the specialized agencies concerned.

2. It may make recommendations for the purpose of promoting respect for, and observance of, human rights and fundamental freedoms for all.

3. It may prepare draft conventions for submission to the General Assembly, with respect to matters falling within its competence.

4. It may call, in accordance with the rules prescribed by the United Nations, international conferences on matters falling within its competence.

Article 63

1. The Economic and Social Council may enter into agreements with any of the agencies referred to in Article 57, defining the terms on which the agency concerned shall be brought into relationship with the United Nations. Such agreements shall be subject to approval by the General Assembly.

2. It may coordinate the activities of the specialized agencies through consultation with and recommendations to such agencies and through recommendations to the General Assembly and to the members of the United Nations.

Article 64

1. The Economic and Social Council may take appropriate steps to obtain regular reports from the specialized agencies. It may make arrangements with the members of the United Nations and with the specialized agencies to obtain reports on the steps taken to give effect to its own recommendations and to recommendations on matters falling within its competence made by the General Assembly.

2. It may communicate its observations on these reports to the General Assembly.

Article 65

The Economic and Social Council may furnish information to the Security Council and shall assist the Security Council upon its request.

Article 66

1. The Economic and Social Council shall perform such functions as fall within its competence in connection with the carrying out of the recommendations of the General Assembly.

2. It may, with the approval of the General Assembly, perform services at the request of members of the United Nations and at the request of specialized agencies.

3. It shall perform such other functions as are specified elsewhere in the present Charter or as may be assigned to it by the General Assembly.

VOTING

Article 67

1. Each member of the Economic and Social Council shall have one vote.

2. Decisions of the Economic and Social Council shall be made by a majority of the members present and voting.

PROCEDURE

Article 68

The Economic and Social Council shall set up commissions in economic and social fields and for the promotion of human rights, and such other commissions as may be required for the performance of its functions.

Article 69

The Economic and Social Council shall invite any member of the United Nations to participate, without vote, in its deliberations on any matter of particular concern to that member.

Article 70

The Economic and Social Council may make arrangements for representatives of the specialized agencies to participate, without vote, in its deliberations and in those of the commissions established by it, and for its representatives to participate in deliberations of the specialized agencies.

Article 71

The Economic and Social Council may make suitable arrangements for consultation with non-governmental organizations which are concerned with matters within its competence. Such arrangements may be made with international organizations and, where appropriate, with national organizations after consultation with the member of the United Nations concerned.

Article 72

1. The Economic and Social Council shall adopt its own rules of procedure, including the method of selecting its President.

2. The Economic and Social Council shall meet as required in accordance with its rules, which shall include provision for the convening of meetings on request of a majority of its members.

CHAPTER XI

DECLARATION REGARDING NON-SELF-GOVERNING TERRITORIES

Article 73

Members of the United Nations which have or assume responsibilities for the administration of territories whose peoples have not yet attained a full measure of self-government recognize the principle that the interests of the inhabitants of these territories are paramount, and accept as a sacred trust the obligation to promote to the utmost, within the system of international peace and security established by the present charter, the well-being of the inhabitants of these territories, and, to this end:

a. To ensure, with due respect for the culture of the peoples concerned, their political, economic, social, and educational advancement, their just treatment, and their protection against abuses;

b. To develop self-government, to take due account of the political aspirations of the peoples, and to assist them in the progressive development of their free political institutions, according to the particular circumstances of each territory and its peoples and their varying stages of advancement;

c. To further international peace and security;

d. To promote constructive measures of development, to encourage research, and to cooperate with one another and, when and where appropriate, with specialized international bodies with a view to the practical achievement of the social, economic, and scientific purposes set forth in this article; and

e. To transmit regularly to the Secretary-General for information purposes, subject to such limitation as security and constitutional considerations may require, statistical and other information of a technical nature relating to economic, social, and educational conditions in the territories for which they are respectively responsible other than those territories to which Chapters XII and XIII apply.

Article 74

Members of the United Nations also agree that their policy in respect of the territories to which this chapter applies, no less than in respect of their metropolitan areas must be based on the general principle of good-neighborliness, due account being taken of the interests and well-being of the rest of the world, in social, economic, and commercial matters.

CHAPTER XII

INTERNATIONAL TRUSTEESHIP SYSTEM

Article 75

The United Nations shall establish under its authority an international trusteeship system for the administration and supervision of such territories as may be placed thereunder by subsequent individual agreements. These territories are hereinafter referred to as trust territories.

Article 76

The basic objectives of the trusteeship system, in accordance with the purposes of the United Nations laid down in Article 1 of the present Charter, shall be:

a. To further international peace and security;

b. To promote the political, economic, social and educational advancement of the inhabitants of the trust territories, and their progressive development towards self-government or independence as may be appropriate to the particular circumstances of each territory and its peoples and the freely expressed wishes of the peoples concerned, and as may be provided by the terms of each trusteeship agreement;

c. To encourage respect for human rights and for fundamental freedoms for all without distinction as to race, sex, language, or religion, and to encourage recognition of the interdependence of the peoples of the world; and

d. To ensure equal treatment in social, economic, and commercial matters for all members of the United Nations and their nationals, and also equal treatment for the latter in the administration of justice, without prejudice to the attainment of the foregoing objectives and subject to the provisions of Article 80.

Article 77

1. The trusteeship system shall apply to such territories in the following categories as may be placed thereunder by means of trusteeship agreements:

a. Territories now held under mandate;

b. Territories which may be detached from enemy states as a result of the Second World War; and

c. Territories voluntarily placed under the system by states responsible for their administration.

2. It will be a matter for subsequent agreement as to which territories in the foregoing categories will be brought under the trusteeship system and upon what terms.

Article 78

The trusteeship system shall not apply to territories which have become members of the United Nations, relationship among which shall be based on respect for the principle of sovereign equality.

Article 79

The terms of trusteeship for each territory to be placed under the trusteeship system, including any alteration or amendment, shall be agreed upon by the states directly concerned, including the mandatory power in the case of territories held under mandate by a member of the United Nations, and shall be approved as provided for in Articles 83 and 85.

Article 80

1. Except as may be agreed upon in individual trusteeship agreements, made under Articles 77, 79, and 81, placing each territory under the trusteeship system, and until such agreements have been concluded, nothing in this chapter shall be construed in or of itself to alter in any manner the rights whatsoever of any states or any peoples or the terms of existing international instruments to which members of the United Nations may respectively be parties.

2. Paragraph 1 of this article shall not be interpreted as giving grounds for delay or postponement of the negotia-

tion and conclusion of agreements for placing mandated and other territories under the trusteeship system as provided for in Article 77.

Article 81

The trusteeship agreement shall in each case include the terms under which the trust territory will be administered and designate the authority which will exercise the administration of the trust territory. Such authority, hereinafter called the administering authority, may be one or more states or the organization itself.

Article 82

There may be designated, in any trusteeship agreement, a strategic area or areas which may include part or all of the trust territory to which the agreement applies, without prejudice to any special agreement or agreements made under Article 43.

Article 83

1. All functions of the United Nations relating to strategic areas, including the approval of the terms of the trusteeship agreements and of their alteration or amendment, shall be exercised by the Security Council.

2. The basic objectives set forth in Article 76 shall be applicable to the people of each strategic area.

3. The Security Council shall, subject to the provisions of the trusteeship agreements and without prejudice to security considerations, avail itself of the assistance of the Trusteeship Council to perform those functions of the United Nations under the trusteeship system relating to political, economic, social, and educational matters in the strategic areas.

Article 84

It shall be the duty of the administering authority to ensure that the trust territory shall play its part in the maintenance of inernational peace and security. To this end the administering authority may make use of volunteer forces, facilities, and assistance from the trust territory in carrying out the obligations towards the Security Council undertaken in this regard by the administering authority, as well as for local defense and the maintenance of law and order within the trust territory.

Article 85

1. The functions of the United Nations with regard to trusteeship agreements for all areas not designated as strategic, including the approval of the terms of the trusteeship agreements and of their alteration or amendment, shall be exercised by the General Assembly.

2. The Trusteeship Council, operating under the authority of the General Assembly, shall assist the General Assembly in carrying out these functions.

CHAPTER XIII

THE TRUSTEESHIP COUNCIL

COMPOSITION

Article 86

1. The Trusteeship Council shall consist of the following members of the United Nations:

a. Those members administering trust territories;

b. Such of those members mentioned by name in Article 23 as are not administering trust territories; and

c. As many other members elected for three-year terms by the General Assembly as may be necessary to ensure that the total number of members of the Trusteeship Council is equally divided between those members of the United Nations which administer trust territories and those which do not.

2. Each member of the Trusteeship Council shall designate one specially qualified person to represent it therein.

FUNCTIONS AND POWERS

Article 87

The General Assembly and, under its authority, the Trusteeship Council, in carrying out their functions, may:

a. Consider reports submitted by the administering authority;

b. Accept petitions and examine them in consultation with the administering authority.

c. Provide for periodic visits to the respective trust territories at times agreed upon with the administering authority; and

d. Take these and other actions in conformity with the terms of the trusteeship agreements.

Article 88

The Trusteeship Council shall formulate a questionnaire on the political, economic, social and educational advancement of the inhabitants of each trust territory, and the administering authority for each trust territory within the competence of the General Assembly shall make an annual report to the General Assembly upon the basis of such questionnaire.

VOTING

Article 89

1. Each member of the Trusteeship Council shall have one vote.

2. Decisions of the Trusteeship Council shall be made by a majority of the members present and voting.

PROCEDURE

Article 90

1. The Trusteeship Council shall adopt its own rules of procedure, including the method of selecting its President.

2. The Trusteeship Council shall meet as required in accordance with its rules, which shall include provision for the convening of meetings on the request of a majority of its members.

Article 91

The Trusteeship Council shall, when appropriate, avail itself of the assistance of the Economic and Social Council and of the specialized agencies in regard to matters with which they are respectively concerned.

CHAPTER XIV

THE INTERNATIONAL COURT OF JUSTICE

Article 92

The International Court of Justice shall be the principal judicial organ of the United Nations. It shall function in accordance with the annexed Statute, which is based upon the Statute of the Permanent Court of International Justice and forms an integral part of the present Charter.

Article 93

1. All members of the United Nations are *ipso facto* parties to the Statute of the International Court of Justice.

2. A state which is not a member of the United Nations may become a party to the Statute of the International Court of Justice on conditions to be determined in each case by the General Assembly upon the recommendation of the Security Council.

Article 94

1. Each member of the United Nations undertakes to comply with the decision of the International Court of Justice in any case to which it is a party.

2. If any party to a case fails to perform the obligations incumbent upon it under a judgment rendered by the Court, the other party may have recourse to the Security Council, which may, if it deems necessary, make recommendations or decide upon measures to be taken to give effect to the judgment.

Article 95

Nothing in the present Charter shall prevent members of the United Nations from entrusting the solution of their differences to other tribunals by virtue of agreements already in existence or which may be concluded in the future.

Article 96

1. The General Assembly or the Security Council may request the International Court of Justice to give an advisory opinion on any legal question.

2. Other organs of the United Nations and specialized agencies, which may at any time be so authorized by the General Assembly, may also request advisory opinions of

the Court on legal questions arising within the scope of their activities.

CHAPTER XV

THE SECRETARIAT

Article 97

The Secretariat shall comprise a Secretary-General and such staff as the organization may require. The Secretary-General shall be appointed by the General Assembly upon the recommendation of the Security Council. He shall be the chief administrative officer of the organization.

Article 98

The Secretary-General shall act in that capacity in all meetings of the General Assembly, of the Security Council, of the Economic and Social Council, and of the Trusteeship Council, and shall perform such other functions as are entrusted to him by these organs. The Secretary-General shall make an annual report to the General Assembly on the work of the organization.

Article 99

The Secretary-General may bring to the attention of the Security Council any matter which in his opinion may threaten the maintenance of international peace and security.

Article 100

1. In the performance of their duties the Secretary-General and the staff shall not seek or receive instructions from any government or from any other authority external to the organization. They shall refrain from any action which might reflect on their position as international officials responsible only to the organization.

2. Each member of the United Nations undertakes to respect the exclusively international character of the responsibilities of the Secretary-General and the staff and not to seek to influence them in the discharge of their responsibilities.

Article 101

1. The staff shall be appointed by the Secretary-General under regulations established by the General Assembly.

2. Appropriate staffs shall be permanently assigned to the Economic and Social Council, the Trusteeship Council, and, as required, to other organs of the United Nations. These staffs shall form a part of the Secretariat.

3. The paramount consideration in the employment of the staff and in the determination of the conditions of service shall be the necessity of securing the highest standards of efficiency, competence, and integrity. Due regard shall be paid to the importance of recruiting the staff on as wide a geographical basis as possible.

CHAPTER XVI

MISCELLANEOUS PROVISIONS

Article 102

1. Every treaty and every international agreement entered into by any member of the United Nations after the present charter comes into force shall as soon as possible be registered with the Secretariat and published by it.

2. No party to any such treaty or international agreement which has not been registered in accordance with the provisions of paragraph 1 of this article may invoke that treaty or agreement before any organ of the United Nations.

Article 103

In the event of a conflict between the obligations of the members of the United Nations under the present Charter and obligations under any other international agreement, their obligations under the present Charter shall prevail.

Article 104

The organization shall enjoy in the territory of each of its members such legal capacity as may be necessary for the exercise of its functions and the fulfillment of its purposes.

Article 105

1. The organization shall enjoy in the territory of each of its members such privileges and immunities as are necessary for the fulfillment of its purposes.

2. Representatives of the members of the United Nations and officials of the organization shall similarly enjoy such privileges and immunities as are necessary for the independent exercise of their functions in connection with the organization.

3. The General Assembly may make recommendations with a view to determining the details of the application of paragraphs 1 and 2 of this article or may propose conventions to the members of the United Nations for this purpose.

CHAPTER XVII

TRANSITIONAL SECURITY ARRANGEMENTS

Article 106

Pending the coming into force of such special agreements referred to in Article 43 as in the opinion of the Security

Council enable it to begin the exercise of its responsibilities under Article 42, the parties to the Four-Nation Declaration, signed at Moscow, October 30, 1943, and France, shall, in accordance with the provisions of paragraph 5 of that Declaration, consult with one another and as occasion requires with other members of the United Nations with a view to such joint action on behalf of the organization as may be necessary for the purpose of maintaining international peace and security.

Article 107

Nothing in the present Charter shall invalidate or preclude action, in relation to any state which during the Second World War has been an enemy of any signatory to the present charter, taken or authorized as a result of that war by the governments having responsibility for such action.

CHAPTER XVIII

AMENDMENTS

Article 108

Amendments to the present Charter shall come into force for all members of the United Nations when they have been adopted by a vote of two-thirds of the members of the General Assembly and ratified in accordance with their respective constitutional processes by two-thirds of the members of the United Nations, including all the permanent members of the Security Council.

Article 109

1. A general conference of the members of the United Nations for the purpose of reviewing the present Charter may be held at a date and place to be fixed by a two-thirds

vote of the members of the General Assembly and by a vote of any seven members of the Security Council. Each member of the United Nations shall have one vote in the conference.

2. Any alteration of the present Charter recommended by a two-thirds vote of the conference shall take effect when ratified in accordance with their respective constitutional processes by two-thirds of the members of the United Nations including all the permanent members of the Security Council.

3. If such a conference has not been held before the tenth annual session of the General Assembly following the coming into force of the present Charter, the proposal to call such a conference shall be placed on the agenda of that session of the General Assembly, and the conference shall be held if so decided by a majority vote of the members of the General Assembly and by a vote of any seven members of the Security Council.

CHAPTER XIX

RATIFICATION AND SIGNATURE

Article 110

1. The present Charter shall be ratified by the signatory states in accordance with their respective constitutional processes.

2. The ratifications shall be deposited with the Government of the United States of America, which shall notify all the signatory states of each deposit as well as the Secretary-General of the organization when he has been appointed.

3. The present Charter shall come into force upon the deposit of ratifications by the Republic of China, France, the

Union of Soviet Socialist Republics, the United Kingdom of Great Britain and Northern Ireland, and the United States of America, and by a majority of the other signatory states. A protocol of the ratifications deposited shall thereupon be drawn up by the Government of the United States of America which shall communicate copies thereof to all the signatory states.

4. The states signatory to the present Charter which ratify it after it has come into force will become original members of the United Nations on the date of the deposit of their respective ratifications.

Article 111

The present Charter, of which the Chinese, French, Russian, English and Spanish texts are equally authentic, shall remain deposited in the archives of the Government of the United States of America. Duly certified copies thereof shall be transmitted by that Government to the Governments of the other signatory states.

In faith whereof the representatives of the Governments of the United Nations have signed the present Charter.

Done at the city of San Francisco the twenty-sixth day of June, one thousand nine hundred and forty-five.

STATUTE OF THE INTERNATIONAL COURT OF JUSTICE *

Article 1

THE International Court of Justice established by the Charter of the United Nations as the principal judicial organ of the United Nations shall be constituted and shall function in accordance with the provisions of the present Statute.

CHAPTER I

ORGANIZATION OF THE COURT

Article 2

The court shall be composed of a body of independent judges, elected regardless of their nationality from among persons of high moral character, who possess the qualifications required in their respective countries for appointment to the highest judicial offices, or are jurisconsults of recognized competence in international law.

Article 3

1. The court shall consist of fifteen members, no two of whom may be nationals of the same state.

2. A person who for the purposes of membership in the

---

* *Charter of the United Nations, Report to the President on the Results of the San Francisco Conference by the Chairman of the United States Delegation, the Secretary of State.* Department of State, Publication 2349, Conference Series 71, Appendix B, p. 238.

court could be regarded as a national of more than one state shall be deemed to be a national of the one in which he ordinarily exercises civil and political rights.

Article 4

1. The members of the court shall be elected by the General Assembly and by the Security Council from a list of persons nominated by the national groups in the Permanent Court of Arbitration, in accordance with the following provisions.

2. In the case of members of the United Nations not represented in the Permanent Court of Arbitration, candidates shall be nominated by national groups appointed for this purpose by their governments under the same conditions as those prescribed for members of the Permanent Court of Arbitration by Article 44 of the Convention of The Hague of 1907 for the pacific settlement of international disputes.

3. The conditions under which a state which is a party to the present Statute but is not a member of the United Nations may participate in electing the members of the Court shall, in the absence of a special agreement, be laid down by the General Assembly upon recommendation of the Security Council.

Article 5

1. At least three months before the date of the election, the Secretary-General of the United Nations shall address a written request to the members of the Permanent Court of Arbitration belonging to the states which are parties to the present Statute, and to the members of the national groups appointed under Article 4, paragraph 2, inviting them to undertake, within a given time, by national groups, the

nomination of persons in a position to accept the duties of a member of the Court.

2. No group may nominate more than four persons, not more than two of whom shall be of their own nationality. In no case may the number of candidates nominated by a group be more than double the number of seats to be filled.

Article 6

Before making these nominations, each national group is recommended to consult its highest court of justice, its legal faculties and schools of law, and its national academies and national sections of international academies devoted to the study of law.

Article 7

1. The Secretary-General shall prepare a list in alphabetical order of all the persons thus nominated. Save as provided in Article 12, paragraph 2, these shall be the only persons eligible.

2. The Secretary-General shall submit this list to the General Assembly and to the Security Council.

Article 8

The General Assembly and the Security Council shall proceed independently of one another to elect the members of the court.

Article 9

At every election, the electors shall bear in mind not only that the persons to be elected should individually possess the qualifications required, but also that in the body as a whole the representation of the main forms of civilization and of the principal legal systems of the world should be assured.

Article 10

1. Those candidates who obtain an absolute majority of votes in the General Assembly and in the Security Council shall be considered as elected.

2. Any vote of the Security Council, whether for the election of judges or for the appointment of members of the conference envisaged in Article 12, shall be taken without any distinction between permanent and non-permanent members of the Security Council.

3. In the event of more than one national of the same state obtaining an absolute majority of the votes both of the General Assembly and of the Security Council, the eldest of these only shall be considered as elected.

Article 11

If, after the first meeting held for the purpose of the election, one or more seats remain to be filled, a second and, if necessary, a third meeting shall take place.

Article 12

1. If, after the third meeting, one or more seats still remain unfilled, a joint conference consisting of six members, three appointed by the General Assembly and three by the Security Council, may be formed at any time at the request of either the General Assembly or the Security Council, for the purpose of choosing by the vote of an absolute majority one name for each seat still vacant, to submit to the General Assembly and the Security Council for their respective acceptance.

2. If the joint conference is unanimously agreed upon any person who fulfills the required conditions, he may be

included in its list, even though he was not included in the list of nominations referred to in Article 7.

3. If the joint conference is satisfied that it will not be successful in procuring an election, those members of the Court who have already been elected shall, within a period to be fixed by the Security Council, proceed to fill the vacant seats by selection from among those candidates who have obtained votes either in the General Assembly or in the Security Council.

4. In the event of an equality of votes among the judges, the eldest judge shall have a casting vote.

Article 13

1. The members of the Court shall be elected for nine years and may be re-elected; provided, however, that of the judges elected at the first election, the terms of five judges shall expire at the end of three years and the terms of five more judges shall expire at the end of six years.

2. The judges whose terms are to expire at the end of the above-mentioned initial periods of three and six years shall be chosen by lot to be drawn by the Secretary-General immediately after the first election has been completed.

3. The members of the Court shall continue to discharge their duties until their places have been filled. Though replaced, they shall finish any cases which they may have begun.

4. In the case of the resignation of a member of the Court, the resignation shall be addressed to the President of the Court for transmission to the Secretary-General. This last notification makes the place vacant.

Article 14

Vacancies shall be filled by the same method as that laid down for the first election, subject to the following provision: the Secretary-General shall, within one month of the occurrence of the vacancy, proceed to issue the invitations provided for in Article 5, and the date of the election shall be fixed by the Security Council.

Article 15

A member of the Court elected to replace a member whose term of office has not expired shall hold office for the remainder of his predecessor's term.

Article 16

1. No member of the Court may exercise any political or administrative function, or engage in any other occupation of a professional nature.

2. Any doubt on this point shall be settled by the decision of the Court.

Article 17

1. No member of the Court may act as agent, counsel, or advocate in any case.

2. No member may participate in the decision of any case in which he has previously taken part as agent, counsel, or advocate for one of the parties, or as a member of a national or international court, or of a commission of inquiry, or in any other capacity.

3. Any doubt on this point shall be settled by the decision of the Court.

Article 18

1. No member of the Court can be dismissed unless, in the unanimous opinion of the other members, he has ceased to fulfill the required conditions.

2. Formal notification thereof shall be made to the Secretary-General by the Registrar.

3. This notification makes the place vacant.

Article 19

The members of the Court, when engaged on the business of the Court, shall enjoy diplomatic privileges and immunities.

Article 20

Every member of the Court shall, before taking up his duties, make a solemn declaration in open court that he will exercise his powers impartially and conscientiously.

Article 21

1. The Court shall elect its President and Vice-President for three years; they may be re-elected.

2. The Court shall appoint its Registrar and may provide for the appointment of such other officers as may be necessary.

Article 22

1. The seat of the Court shall be established at The Hague. This, however, shall not prevent the Court from sitting and exercising its functions elsewhere whenever the Court considers it desirable.

2. The President and the Registrar shall reside at the seat of the Court.

Article 23

1. The Court shall remain permanently in session, except during the judicial vacations, the dates and duration of which shall be fixed by the Court.

2. Members of the Court are entitled to periodic leave, the dates and duration of which shall be fixed by the Court, having in mind the distance between The Hague and the home of each judge.

3. Members of the Court shall be bound, unless they are on leave or prevented from attending by illness or other serious reasons duly explained to the President, to hold themselves permanently at the disposal of the Court.

Article 24

1. If, for some special reason, a member of the Court considers that he should not take part in the decision of a particular case, he shall so inform the President.

2. If the President considers that for some special reason one of the members of the Court should not sit in a particular case, he shall give him notice accordingly.

3. If in any such case the member of the Court and the President disagree, the matter shall be settled by the decision of the Court.

Article 25

1. The full Court shall sit except when it is expressly provided otherwise in the present Statute.

2. Subject to the condition that the number of judges available to constitute the Court is not thereby reduced below eleven, the rules of the Court may provide for allowing one or more judges, according to circumstances and in rotation, to be dispensed from sitting.

3. A quorum of nine judges shall suffice to constitute the Court.

Article 26

1. The Court may from time to time form one or more chambers, composed of three or more judges as the Court may determine, for dealing with particular categories of cases; for example, labor cases and cases relating to transit and communications.

2. The Court may at any time form a chamber for dealing with a particular case. The number of judges to constitute such a chamber shall be determined by the Court with the approval of the parties.

3. Cases shall be heard and determined by the chambers provided for in this Article if the parties so request.

Article 27

A judgment given by any of the chambers provided for in Articles 26 and 29 shall be considered as rendered by the Court.

Article 28

The chambers provided for in Articles 26 and 29 may, with the consent of the parties, sit and exercise their functions elsewhere than at The Hague.

Article 29

With a view to the speedy despatch of business, the Court shall form annually a chamber composed of five judges which, at the request of the parties, may hear and determine cases by summary procedure. In addition, two judges shall be selected for the purpose of replacing judges who find it impossible to sit.

Article 30

1. The Court shall frame rules for carrying out its functions. In particular, it shall lay down rules of procedure.

2. The rules of the Court may provide for assessors to sit with the Court or with any of its chambers, without the right to vote.

Article 31

1. Judges of the nationality of each of the parties shall retain their right to sit in the case before the Court.

2. If the Court includes upon the bench a judge of the nationality of one of the parties, any other party may choose a person to sit as judge. Such person shall be chosen preferably from among those persons who have been nominated as candidates as provided in Articles 4 and 5.

3. If the Court includes upon the bench no judge of the nationality of the parties, each of these parties may proceed to choose a judge as provided in paragraph 2 of this Article.

4. The provisions of this Article shall apply to the case of Articles 26 and 29. In such cases, the President shall request one or, if necessary, two of the members of the Court forming the chamber to give place to the members of the Court of the nationality of the parties concerned, and, failing such, or if they are unable to be present, to the judges specially chosen by the parties.

5. Should there be several parties in the same interest, they shall, for the purpose of the preceding provisions, be reckoned as one party only. Any doubt upon this point shall be settled by the decision of the Court.

6. Judges chosen as laid down in paragraphs 2, 3, and 4, of this Article shall fulfill the conditions required by Articles 2, 17 (paragraph 2), 20, and 24 of the present Statute.

They shall take part in the decision on terms of complete equality with their colleagues.

Article 32

1. Each member of the Court shall receive an annual salary.

2. The President shall receive a special annual allowance.

3. The Vice-President shall receive a special allowance for every day on which he acts as President.

4. The judges chosen under Article 31, other than members of the Court, shall receive compensation for each day on which they exercise their functions.

5. These salaries, allowances, and compensation shall be fixed by the General Assembly. They may not be decreased during the term of office.

6. The salary of the Registrar shall be fixed by the General Assembly on the proposal of the Court.

7. Regulations made by the General Assembly shall fix the conditions under which retirement pensions may be given to members of the Court and to the Registrar, and the conditions under which members of the Court and the Registrar shall have their traveling expenses refunded.

8. The above salaries, allowances, and compensations shall be free of all taxation.

Article 33

The expenses of the Court shall be borne by the United Nations in such a manner as shall be decided by the General Assembly.

CHAPTER II

COMPETENCE OF THE COURT

Article 34

1. Only states may be parties in cases before the Court.

2. The Court, subject to and in conformity with its Rules, may request of public international organizations information relevant to cases before it, and shall receive such information presented by such organizations on their own initiative.

3. Whenever the construction of the constituent instrument of a public international organization or of an international convention adopted thereunder is in question in a case before the Court, the Registrar shall so notify the public international organization concerned and shall communicate to it copies of all the written proceedings.

Article 35

1. The Court shall be open to the states parties to the present Statute.

2. The conditions under which the Court shall be open to other states shall, subject to the special provisions contained in treaties in force, be laid down by the Security Council, but in no case shall such conditions place the parties in a position of inequality before the Court.

3. When a state which is not a member of the United Nations is a party to a case, the Court shall fix the amount which that party is to contribute towards the expenses of the Court. This provision shall not apply if such state is bearing a share of the expenses of the Court.

Article 36

1. The jurisdiction of the Court comprises all cases which the parties refer to it and all matters especially provided for in the Charter of the United Nations or in treaties and conventions in force.

2. The states parties to the present Statute may at any time declare that they recognize as compulsory *ipso facto* and without special agreement, in relation to any other state accepting the same obligation, the jurisdiction of the Court in all legal disputes concerning:

a. The interpretation of a treaty;

b. Any question of international law;

c. The existence of any fact which, if established, would constitute a breach of an international obligation;

d. The nature or extent of the reparation to be made for the breach of an international obligation.

3. The declarations referred to above may be made unconditionally or on condition of reciprocity on the part of several or certain states, or for a certain time.

4. Such declarations shall be deposited with the Secretary-General of the United Nations, who shall transmit copies thereof to the parties to the statute and to the Registrar of the Court.

5. Declarations made under Article 36 of the Statute of the Permanent Court of International Justice and which are still in force shall be deemed, as between the parties to the present Statute, to be acceptances of the compulsory jurisdiction of the International Court of Justice for the period which they still have to run and in accordance with their terms.

6. In the event of a dispute as to whether the Court has

jurisdiction, the matter shall be settled by the decision of the Court.

Article 37

Whenever a treaty or convention in force provides for reference of a matter to a tribunal to have been instituted by the League of Nations, or to the Permanent Court of International Justice, the matter shall, as between the parties to the present Statute, be referred to the International Court of Justice.

Article 38

1. The Court, whose function is to decide in accordance with international law such disputes as are submitted to it, shall apply:

a. International conventions, whether general or particular, establishing rules expressly recognized by the contesting states;

b. International custom, as evidence of a general practice accepted as law;

c. The general principles of law recognized by civilized nations;

d. Subject to the provisions of Article 59, judicial decisions and the teachings of the most highly qualified publicists of the various nations, as subsidiary means for the determination of rules of law.

2. This provision shall not prejudice the power of the court to decide a case *ex æquo et bono,* if the parties agree thereto.

CHAPTER III

PROCEDURE

Article 39

1. The official languages of the Court shall be French and English. If the parties agree that the case shall be conducted in French, the judgment shall be delivered in French. If the parties agree that the case shall be conducted in English, the judgment shall be delivered in English.

2. In the absence of an agreement as to which language shall be employed, each party may, in the pleadings, use the language which it prefers; the decision of the Court shall be given in French and English. In this case the Court shall at the same time determine which of the two texts shall be considered as authoritative.

3. The Court shall, at the request of any party, authorize a language other than French or English to be used by that party.

Article 40

1. Cases are brought before the Court, as the case may be, either by the notification of the special agreement or by a written application addressed to the Registrar. In either case the subject of the dispute and the parties shall be indicated.

2. The Registrar shall forthwith communicate the application to all concerned.

3. He shall also notify the members of the United Nations through the Secretary-General, and also any other states entitled to appear before the Court.

Article 41

1. The Court shall have the power to indicate, if it considers that circumstances so require, any provisional measures which ought to be taken to preserve the respective rights of either party.

2. Pending the final decision, notice of the measures suggested shall forthwith be given to the parties and to the Security Council.

Article 42

1. The parties shall be represented by agents.

2. They may have the assistance of counsel or advocates before the Court.

3. The agents, counsel, and advocates of parties before the Court shall enjoy the privileges and immunities necessary to the independent exercise of their duties.

Article 43

1. The procedure shall consist of two parts: written and oral.

2. The written proceedings shall consist of the communication to the Court and to the parties of memorials, countermemorials and, if necessary, replies; also all papers and documents in support.

3. These communications shall be made through the Registrar, in the order and within the time fixed by the Court.

4. A certified copy of every document produced by one party shall be communicated to the other party.

5. The oral proceedings shall consist of the hearings by the Court of witnesses, experts, agents, counsel, and advocates.

Article 44

1. For the service of all notices upon persons other than the agents, counsel, and advocates, the Court shall apply direct to the government of the state upon whose territory the notice has to be served.

2. The same provision shall apply whenever steps are to be taken to procure evidence on the spot.

Article 45

The hearing shall be under the control of the President or, if he is unable to preside, of the Vice-President; if neither is able to preside, the senior judge present shall preside.

Article 46

The hearing in Court shall be public, unless the Court shall decide otherwise, or unless the parties demand that the public be not admitted.

Article 47

1. Minutes shall be made at each hearing and signed by the Registrar and the President.

2. These minutes alone shall be authentic.

Article 48

The Court shall make orders for the conduct of the case, shall decide the form and time in which each party must conclude its arguments, and make all arrangements connected with the taking of evidence.

Article 49

The Court may, even before the hearing begins, call upon the agents to produce any document or to supply any explanations. Formal note shall be taken of any refusal.

Article 50

The Court may, at any time, entrust any individual, body, bureau, commission, or other organization that it may select, with the task of carrying out an inquiry or giving an expert opinion.

Article 51

During the hearing any relevant questions are to be put to the witnesses and experts under the conditions laid down by the Court in the rules of procedure referred to in Article 30.

Article 52

After the Court has received the proofs and evidence within the time specified for the purpose, it may refuse to accept any further oral or written evidence that one party may desire to present unless the other side consents.

Article 53

1. Whenever one of the parties does not appear before the Court, or fails to defend its case, the other party may call upon the Court to decide in favor of its claim.

2. The Court must, before doing so, satisfy itself, not only that it has jurisdiction in accordance with Articles 36 and 37, but also that the claim is well founded in fact and law.

Article 54

1. When, subject to the control of the Court, the agents, counsel, and advocates have completed their presentation of the case, the President shall declare the hearing closed.

2. The Court shall withdraw to consider the judgment.

3. The deliberations of the Court shall take place in private and remain secret.

Article 55

1. All questions shall be decided by a majority of the judges present.

2. In the event of an equality of votes, the President or the judge who acts in his place shall have a casting vote.

Article 56

1. The judgment shall state the reasons on which it is based.

2. It shall contain the names of the judges who have taken part in the decision.

Article 57

If the judgment does not represent in whole or in part the unanimous opinion of the judges, any judge shall be entitled to deliver a separate opinion.

Article 58

The judgment shall be signed by the President and by the Registrar. It shall be read in open court, due notice having been given to the agents.

Article 59

The decision of the Court has no binding force except between the parties and in respect of that particular case.

Article 60

The judgment is final and without appeal. In the event of dispute as to the meaning or scope of the judgment, the Court shall construe it upon the request of any party.

Article 61

1. An application for revision of a judgment may be made only when it is based upon the discovery of some fact of such a nature as to be a decisive factor, which fact was, when the judgment was given, unknown to the Court and also to the party claiming revision, always provided that such ignorance was not due to negligence.

2. The proceedings for revision shall be opened by a judgment of the Court expressly recording the existence of the new fact, recognizing that it has such a character as to lay the case open to revision, and declaring the application admissible on this ground.

3. The Court may require previous compliance with the terms of the judgment before it admits proceedings in revision.

4. The application for revision must be made at latest within six months of the discovery of the new fact.

5. No application for revision may be made after the lapse of ten years from the date of the judgment.

Article 62

1. Should a state consider that it has an interest of a legal nature which may be affected by the decision in the case, it may submit a request to the Court to be permitted to intervene.

2. It shall be for the Court to decide upon this request.

Article 63

1. Whenever the construction of a convention to which states other than those concerned in the case are parties is

in question, the Registrar shall notify all such states forth-with.

2. Every state so notified has the right to intervene in the proceedings, but if it uses this right, the construction given by the judgment will be equally binding upon it.

Article 64

Unless otherwise decided by the Court, each party shall bear its own costs.

CHAPTER IV

ADVISORY OPINIONS

Article 65

1. The Court may give an advisory opinion on any legal question at the request of whatever body may be authorized by or in accordance with the Charter of the United Nations to make such a request.

2. Questions upon which the advisory opinion of the Court is asked shall be laid before the Court by means of a written request containing an exact statement of the question upon which an opinion is required, and accompanied by all documents likely to throw light upon the question.

Article 66

1. The Registrar shall forthwith give notice of the request for an advisory opinion to all states entitled to appear before the Court.

2. The Registrar shall also, by means of a special and direct communication, notify any state entitled to appear before the Court or international organization considered by the Court, or, should it not be sitting, by the President, as likely

to be able to furnish information on the question, that the court will be prepared to receive, within a time limit to be fixed by the President, written statements, or to hear, at a public sitting to be held for the purpose, oral statements relating to the question.

3. Should any such state entitled to appear before the Court have failed to receive the special communication referred to in paragraph 2 of this Article, such state may express a desire to submit a written statement or to be heard; and the Court will decide.

4. States and organizations having presented written or oral statements or both shall be permitted to comment on the statements made by other states or organizations in the form, to the extent, and within the time limits which the Court, or, should it not be sitting, the President, shall decide in each particular case. Accordingly, the Registrar shall in due time communicate any such written statements to states and organizations having submitted similar statements.

Article 67

The Court shall deliver its advisory opinions in open court, notice having been given to the Secretary-General and to the representatives of members of the United Nations, of other states and of international organizations immediately concerned.

Article 68

In the exercise of its advisory functions the Court shall further be guided by the provisions of the present Statute which apply in contentious cases to the extent to which it recognizes them to be applicable.

CHAPTER V

AMENDMENT

Article 69

Amendments to the present Statute shall be effected by the same procedure as is provided by the Charter of the United Nations for amendments to that Charter, subject however to any provisions which the General Assembly upon recommendation of the Security Council may adopt concerning the participation of states which are parties to the present Statute but are not members of the United Nations.

Article 70

The Court shall have power to propose such amendments to the present Statute as it may deem necessary, through written communications to the Secretary-General, for consideration in conformity with the provisions of Article 69.

INDEX

A

Alexander, Field Marshal, 169
Anglo-Soviet Treaty, 185-188
Antonov, Army General, 170
Arab League, 55, 90
Argentina, 44, 46
    admission to the United Nations, 54, 58, 59
    declaration of war on Japan and Germany, 51-52
    Farrell government, 40-41, 52, 121
Atlantic Charter, 28
Atomic bomb, 110, 114, 116, 117
Austin, Warren, 40, 45
Australia, at San Francisco Conference, 63

B

Berlin Conference, 104-109
    German policy of, 104-108
Bevin, Foreign Secretary, 119-121
Bidault, Georges, 61, 62
Bilateral security, 94-95
Bohlen, Charles E., 169
Borah, William E., 128
Braden, Spruille, 122
Briand, Aristide, 23

Bridges, Sir Edward, 169
British Commonwealth Conference, 62
Brooke, Sir Alan, 169
Buenos Aires Peace Conference of 1936, 46
Byrnes, James F., 168

C

Cadogan, Sir Alexander, 1, 72, 169
Canada, at San Francisco Conference, 63
Chapultepec, Act of, 45, 46, 50, 94-95, 179-184
    principles of, 42-43
Chiang Kai-shek, 19, 111, 113
China, settlement with Russia, 111-113
Chinese Changchun Railway, 112
Chinese Eastern Railway, 112
Churchill, Winston, 25, 26, 70, 85, 109, 119, 120, 168, 178
Ciano, Count, 108
Clark-Kerr, Sir Archibald, 30, 169, 175
Colonies, American public opinion on, 87-88

Congress of Vienna, 66
Connally, Tom, 40, 45, 64, 101
Crimea Conference (*see* Yalta Conference)
Cunningham, Sir Andrew, 169
Czechoslovakia, treaty with Russia, 192-195

D

Democracy, furtherance of, 120
Dewey, Thomas E., 20
Dumbarton Oaks Conference, 1-24, 32
  criticism of, 11-24, 75
  ten key points, 1-5
  two phases of, 1, 149
Dumbarton Oaks documents on international organization. Report to the Secretary of State, 149-150
  proposals, 151-167
  Statement by the President of the United States regarding the Dumbarton Oaks Proposals, 145-147
  Statement by the Secretary of State, 147-149
  Statement issued simultaneously by the participating governments, 151

E

Economic Charter of the Americas, 41
Eden, Anthony, 57, 72, 169
Eisenhower, General Dwight D., 18

England, treaty with the Soviet Union (May 26, 1942), 185-188
Evatt, Dr. Herbert V., 63, 71, 79

F

Fierlinger, Zdenek, 192, 195
Foreign policy, reforms in, essential in United States, 130
  voters' effect on, 133-134
Foreign Policy Association, 19
Foreign Secretaries, meetings of, 177
France, at the San Francisco Conference, 60-61, 68-69
  treaty with Russia, 189-191
Franco-Soviet Alliance, 189-191
Fraser, Peter, 63
Fulbright, J. William, 131

G

Germany, Berlin Conference policy on, 104-108
  Yalta Conference policy on, 26-27
Gromyko, Andrei, 1, 170
Groza, Premier, 29
Gusev, F. T., 170

H

Harriman, W. Averell, 30, 169, 175
Havana Declaration of 1940, 46
Hay, John, 128
Hiss, Alger, 169
Hitler, Adolf, 146

Hopkins, Harry, 73, 168
Hull, Cordell, 132, 137
    Statement regarding Dumbarton
        Oaks Proposals, 147-149

I

Ideals, 135-136
India at the San Francisco Confer-
    ence, 63
Inter-American Conference on War
    and Peace, 39, 182-184
International Labor Office, 100
Ismay, Sir Hastings, 169

J

Jackson, Robert H., 115
Japan, acceptance of peace terms,
    110-111
    ultimatum to, 109-111

K

Khudyakov, Marshal of Aviation,
    170
King, Fleet Admiral Ernest J., 168
Koo, V. K. Wellington, 1
Kurile Islands, 113
Kuter, L. S., 168
Kuznetsov, Admiral, 169

L

Land, Admiral Emory S., 168
League of Nations, 5-10, 25, 34,
    58, 63, 66, 100, 128, 138
Leahy, Fleet Admiral William D.,
    168
Leathers, Lord, 169
Lend-Lease termination, 119

M

MacArthur, General of Army, 110,
    122
Maiski, I. M., 170
Manchuria, 112
Manuilsky, M., 59
Mao Tse-tung, 111
Marshall, General of Army, George
    168
Matthews, H. Freeman, 169
Mexico City Conference, 33, 39-52
    acts of aggression covered by, 43
    objections to the Dumbarton
        Oaks Proposals, 48
Molotov, V. M., 30, 37, 54, 58,
    59, 65, 113, 169, 175, 192,
    195
Monroe Doctrine, 43, 94, 124
Morse, Wayne, 131
Moscow Declaration, 6
Mountbatten, Lord Louis, 18
Myrdal, Gunnar, 117

N

New Zealand at San Francisco Con-
    ference, 63

O

"Open Door" policy, 124
Outer Mongolia, 112

P

Pan-American Society, 121
Pan American Union, 4, 39, 50,
    51, 52, 58
    changes in, 51
Paris Peace Conference, 25, 101

Parra-Perez, Foreign Minister of Venezuela, 48

Permanent Court of International Justice, 5, 9, 96, 98, 128

Pétain, Henri Philippe, 108

Peter, King of Yugoslavia, 32

Poland, Yalta Conference policy on, 29-31, 175-176

Polish Provisional Government of National Unity, 30, 175

Portal, Sir Charles, 169

Potsdam Declaration, 104-109

R

Reciprocal Assistance and American Solidarity, Declaration on, 42, 179-184

Regional security, 20-22, 42-43, 163-164, 179-184, 215-217
relationship of, to collective security, 93

Reorganization, Consolidation and Strengthening of the Inter-American System, Resolution on, 42, 50

Reynaud, Paul, 108

Rockefeller, Nelson, 121, 122

Roosevelt, Franklin D., 19, 25, 26, 36, 70, 84, 85, 135, 168, 178
Statement regarding the Dumbarton Oaks Proposals, 145-147

Russia, critical attitude toward San Francisco Conference, 55-57
declaration of war on Japan, 110

Russia, initiative at the San Francisco Conference, 64-65
treaty with Czechoslovakia, 192-195
treaty with France 189-191
treaty with the United Kingdom (May 26, 1942), 185-188
voting strength in United Nations Organization, 58-59

Russian-Czechoslovak Mutual Assistance Treaty, 192-195

Russo-Chinese settlement, 111

S

Sakhalin, 113

Saltonstall, Leverett, 131

San Francisco Conference, 53-103
Dumbarton Oaks Proposals retained, 67
Economic and Social Cooperation, Committee on, 63
nations represented, 53 n.
political overtones, 54-55
predominance of non-European countries, 59-61
Russia, critical attitude toward, 55-57
Russian initiative, 64-65
veto power controversy, 70-74

Sarnoff, David, 116

Senate Foreign Relations Committee, 128, 132

Sinkiang, 113

Smith, H. Alexander, 131

Smuts, Marshal Jan, 75

Sofianopoulos, John, 61
Somervell, General Brehon B., 168
Somerville, Admiral, 169
Soong, T. V., 57
South Manchuria Railway, 112
Spaak, Foreign Minister, 61
Stalin, Joseph, 19, 25, 26, 29, 36, 37, 70, 73, 112, 168, 178
Stassen, Commander Harold E., 64
Stettinius, Edward R., Jr., 1, 33, 35, 37, 40, 47, 51, 64, 99, 102, 168
  Report to the Secretary of State on Dumbarton Oaks Proposals, 150
Subasitch, Dr., 32, 176

T

Tito, Marshal, 32, 61, 176
Treaties, ratification of, 127
Treaty of Versailles, 25
Truman, Harry S., 57, 97, 99, 102, 110, 116, 130
Trust territories, 88, 225

U

United Nations, 2, 28, 151
  action with respect to threats to the peace, breaches of the peace, and acts of aggression, 160-164, 211-216
  comparison with League of Nations, 5-10, 34, 66, 68, 69, 79, 90, 91, 92-93, 96
  criticism of, 11-24, 102, 114

United Nations, declaration of, regarding Non-self-governing Territories, 223-224
Economic and Social Council, 7, 9, 10, 14, 63, 103, 164, 217-223
  composition, 165, 219
  functions and powers, 82-84, 165-166, 220-221
  objectives, 83, 164
  procedure, 166
  voting, 165, 222-223
General Assembly, 2, 3, 7, 14, 26, 35, 36, 37, 38, 48, 49, 50, 58-59, 67, 103, 153-156, 200-205
  changes made in, at San Francisco, 78-82
  composition, 153, 200-201
  functions and powers, 78-82, 154-155, 201-204
  procedure, 156, 205
  relation of, to Security Council, 78-82
  voting, 155-156, 204-205
  as world forum, 78-82
International Court of Justice, 95-97, 102, 103, 158-159, 230-232
  advisory opinions, 258-259
  competence, 249-251
  organization, 238-248
  procedure, 252-258
  statute, 238-260
membership in, 153, 199-200
  withdrawal from, 98

United Nations, Mexico City Conference proposals, 48-49

Military Staff Committee, 4, 10, 68, 95, 162-163, 214

pacific settlement of disputes, 159-164, 209-211

Preparatory Commission, 99-100

principal organs, 153, 200

purposes and principles of, 76-77, 152-153, 197-199

Secretariat, 166-167, 232-233

Security Council, 1-4, 8-9, 14, 17-21, 26, 33, 35, 37, 48-50, 58, 61, 67-72, 79, 102, 156-158, 206-209

composition, 156-158, 206

functions and powers, 157, 206-207

procedure, 158, 208-209

voting, 33-38, 70, 157, 207-208

transitional arrangements, 167, 234-235

Trusteeship Council, 91-92, 228-230

composition, 228-229

functions and powers, 229

procedure, 230

voting, 230

trusteeship system, 84-93, 224-228

objectives, 88, 225

territories under, 89-91, 225-227

United States attitude toward, 100

United Nations, Yalta Conference Proposals, 172-173

United Nations Charter, 76-77, 151, 196-237

amendments, 97-98, 167, 235-236

criticism, 74

Dumbarton Oaks proposals retained, 67, 74-75

miscellaneous provisions, 233-234

not ideal, 65-66

ratification, 236-237

ratified by U. S. Senate, 101

United Nations, Conference on International Organization, 53-103

United Nations War Crimes Commission, 115

United States, attitude of, toward United Nations, 100

role of, at the San Francisco Conference, 63

UNRRA, 129

V

Van Kleffens, Foreign Minister, 61

Vandenberg, Senator Arthur, 63-64, 101

Versailles Treaty, 128

Voters, effect of, on foreign policy, 133-134, 138-141

rights of, 136-138

Vyshinski, A. Y., 170

W

Washington, George, 135, 136
Willkie, Wendell L., 16
Wilson, Field Marshal, 169
Wilson, Woodrow, 128, 133
World federation, prospects of a, 22-24

Y

Yalta Conference, 25-38
  meetings of Foreign Secretaries, 177

Yalta Conference, policy of, on Germany, 26-27, 170-172
  on liberated Europe, 28-29, 173-175
  on Poland, 29-31, 175-176
  on Yugoslavia, 31-32, 176-177
  Report of the, 168-178
  United Nations Conference proposed, 172-173
Yugoslavia, Yalta Conference policy, 31-32